my first animal encyclopedia

An imprint of Sterling Publishing
387 Park Avenue South
New York, NY 10016

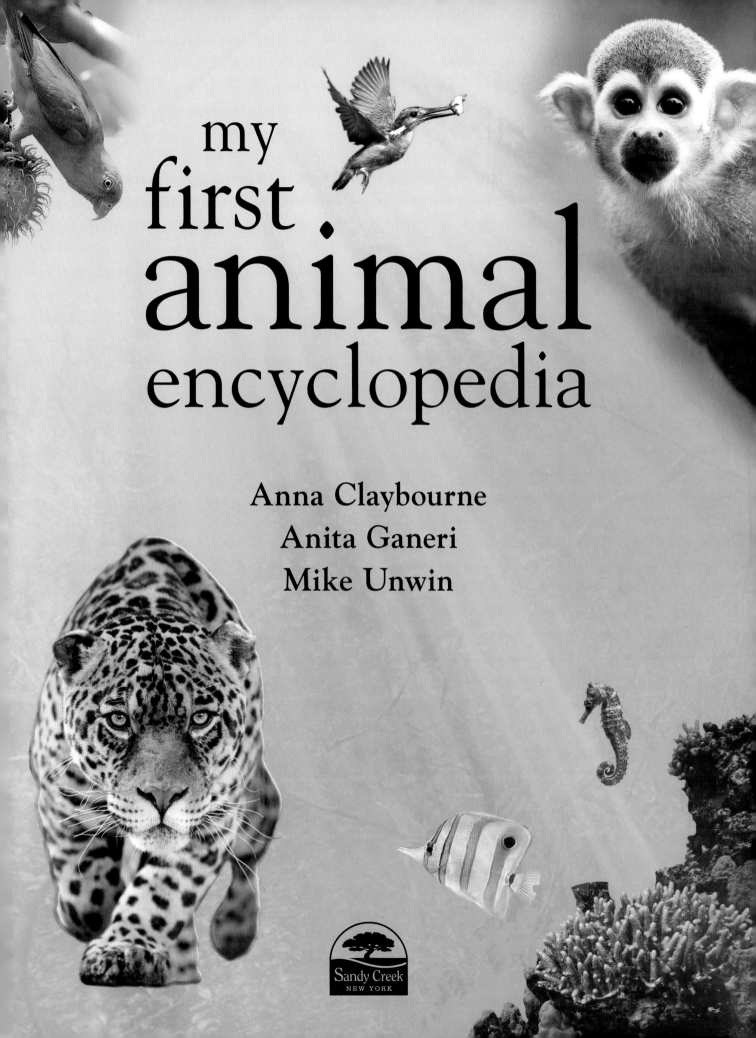

my
first
animal
encyclopedia

Anna Claybourne

Anita Ganeri

Mike Unwin

Sandy Creek
NEW YORK

Contents

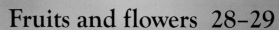

Rainforest life

Tropical rainforests grow along the equator, where it is hot, rainy, and steamy all year round. They are home to millions of animals—more than anywhere else on Earth. Animals can find lots of food here, as well as many hiding places.

North America

Europe

Asia

Southeast Asia

India

The Philippines

Equator

Africa

Brazil

Sumatra

Borneo

New Guinea

South America

Australia

Madagascar

◀ The tropical parts of the world are found to the north and south of the equator.

▲ The rainforests are shown in green.

Blooming forests

Rainforests grow mainly in India and Southeast Asia, West and Central Africa, and South America. There are also patches along the northeast coast of Australia and in New Guinea. The biggest rainforest grows along the banks of the Amazon River in Brazil.

Warm and wet

It always feels warm and sticky in the rainforest, with temperatures reaching around 77°F during the day and at night. It rains almost every day—at least 75 inches of rain falling every year.

Rainforests cover only about a sixth of the Earth's surface. But they are home to half of all the world's known species of animals, more than any other habitat.

▲ A baby orangutan learns how to swing through the trees.

Forest layers

Rainforest trees grow in layers, depending on how tall they are. The tallest are the emergents, which tower above everything. Below them is the canopy. Underneath is the understory—and then, finally, the dark and gloomy forest floor. Each layer has its own particular types of plants and animals.

◄ Toucans are famous for their brightly colored beaks.

► Ants are the most common rainforest animals. These leaf-cutter ants are collecting materials to take back to their nest.

High in the treetops

Towering throughout the rainforest is a scattering of giant trees, called emergents. They can grow to more than 200ft tall—that's as high as a 20-story building! Even though they are often battered by howling winds, they are still home to many different types of animals.

Swooping eagles

A harpy eagle from South America perches on a branch, on the lookout for food. When it spots a sloth or a howler monkey, it swoops down at high speed and grabs its prey with its huge talons (claws).

▲ Emergent trees stretch upward, many feet into the air.

▶ Harpy eagles build their nests high up in the trees.

▶ A colugo resting on a tree trunk, with its "wings" folded away.

◀ This agile spider monkey is hanging by its tail.

Super gliders

Colugos live in the rainforests of Southeast Asia, where they glide among the emergent trees. They are the size of squirrels and their legs are joined by folds of furry skin. They stretch out their legs to use these folds as wings.

AWESOME!

The tallest trees in the rainforest are tualang trees. They grow in Southeast Asia and can reach a dizzy 295ft in height! There are no branches growing on these trees until about halfway up their trunks.

Spider monkeys

These monkeys spend their lives in the treetops of South America, searching for fruit to eat. They get their name from their long, spindly, spiderlike arms and legs. Expert climbers, they use their long tails to grab onto branches and swing from one to another.

Under the canopy

The canopy stretches out beneath the emergent trees like a thick, green roof of leaves. It bursts with life and color, and is home to two thirds of the rainforest's animals and plants.

Howler monkeys

Every morning in the Amazon rainforest, in South America, groups of howler monkeys howl and shriek. The noise is ear-splitting and can be heard from up to three miles away. It warns other monkeys to stay away from their patch of forest.

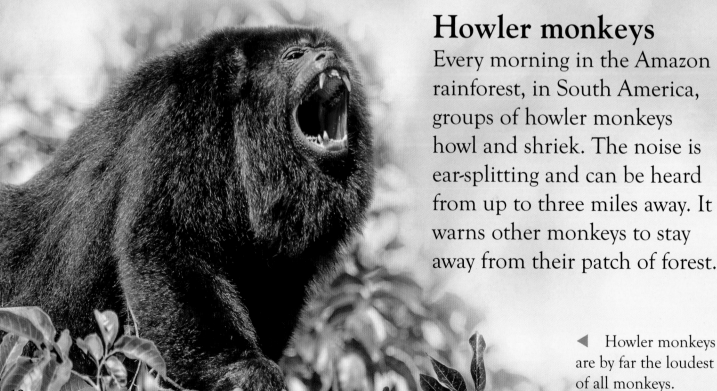

◀ Howler monkeys are by far the loudest of all monkeys.

Tree frogs

Tiny red-eyed tree frogs live in the canopy layer. They lay their eggs on leaves above rivers or ponds. When the tadpoles hatch, they drop straight down into the water and swim away.

▶ Sunbirds live in the rainforests of Africa and Asia.

AWESOME!

Toucans use their famously long, brightly colored beaks to reach fruit growing on branches that are too small to take their weight.

Sunbird snacks

Sunbirds feed on sweet nectar from the rainforest flowers. They perch on a branch and use their long, downward-curving bills to reach deep inside a flower. They also eat insects and spiders.

▼ The southern tamandua—also known as the collared anteater—uses its claws for breaking open insect nests.

Tamanduas

The southern tamandua climbs through the canopy at night, looking for ants and termites to eat. It licks up the insects with its long tongue. It has long claws for clinging onto branches, and can curl its tail around trees for extra grip.

The understory

Small trees, such as spindly palms and saplings, grow in the understory, below the canopy. Here it is hot, damp, and gloomy, as much of the light is blocked by the layers of leaves and branches above.

▶ The branches and trunks of the trees here are covered in trailing vines and creepers. These are often used by animals as climbing ropes.

Sneaky snakes

Some understory snakes are long, green, and slender—and look like vines dangling from the trees. The vine snake sits on a branch, waiting for a lizard or mouse to pass by, then it strikes. By the time its prey spots the snake, it is too late to escape.

◀ Vine snakes also have heads shaped like leaves, making them very hard to spot.

14

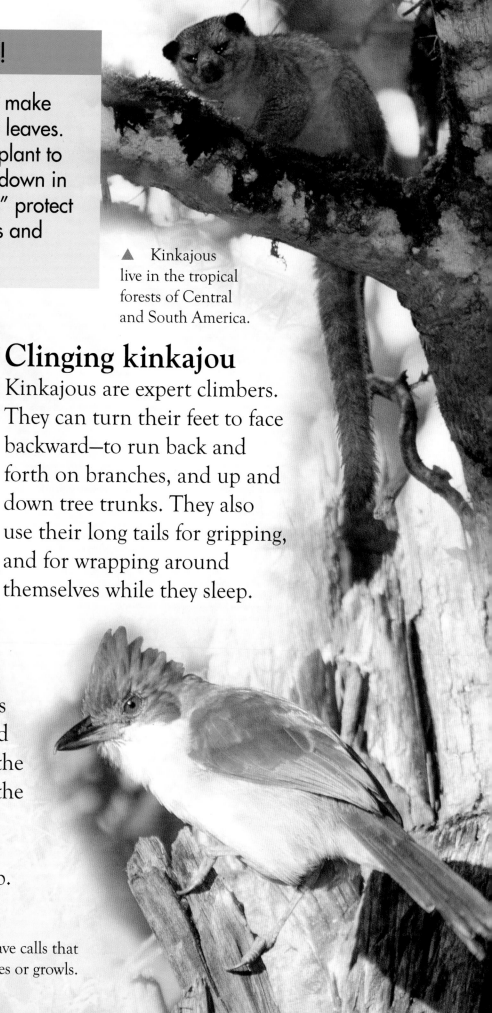

▲ Kinkajous live in the tropical forests of Central and South America.

▲ These tent-making bats are safe in the shelter they have made.

Clinging kinkajou

Kinkajous are expert climbers. They can turn their feet to face backward—to run back and forth on branches, and up and down tree trunks. They also use their long tails for gripping, and for wrapping around themselves while they sleep.

Ant birds

Antshrikes are rainforest birds that build their nests in the understory, but feed on insects and lizards on the forest floor. Some follow the armies of ants that march across the forest floor and eat the insects they disturb.

▶ Antshrikes have calls that sound like chuckles or growls.

▲ The bushmaster's coloring and patterns help it to catch its prey by surprise.

Forest floor

Very little sunlight reaches the gloomy forest floor. A thick layer of roots, twigs, and rotting leaves covers the ground. This is where a huge number of animals live and feed.

Masters of disguise

▼ Rotting leaves and plants put goodness back into the soil.

Bushmasters are large, venomous snakes from Central and South America. They can grow up to 10ft long and have markings that blend with the forest floor, making them difficult to spot. When they are lying still, they look exactly like a harmless pile of leaves.

AWESOME!

The royal antelopes of West Africa are shy, secretive, and hard to spot. They are roughly the same size as rabbits, with legs as thin as pencils.

Hissing cockroach

This creepy cockroach lives on the island of Madagascar, off Africa, where it shelters under logs and leaves on the forest floor. When it is disturbed, it makes a hissing sound by squeezing air out of tiny holes in its body.

▶ Its brown color hides the cockroach among leaves and trees.

Tapir trails

Tapirs eat fruit and leaves, which they search for in the morning and evening gloom. They follow well worn paths through the forest to find the best fruit trees.

◀ The Malayan tapir's black-and-white coat helps to disguise it in patches of light and shade.

Rainforest rivers

Flowing through the rainforest are large rivers and small streams. They are home to thousands of animals. Some swim in the water, while others come to feed and drink. Others live among plants and burrows along the banks.

AWESOME!

The amazing matamata turtle lurks on the riverbed, looking like a rock and waiting for prey to pass by. It uses its very long snout—like a snorkel—to reach the surface so that it can still breathe while it is underwater.

▲ A flap of skin between its legs helps the bat to scoop fish out of the water.

Fishing bats

The fishing bat swoops low over the water, using echolocation to detect ripples made by fish. Then it uses its sharp, hooked claws to fish its prey out of the water. It eats its food as it flies or carries it to a nearby tree or cave.

Water dragons

Water dragons are lizards that live by rivers in Australia and Southeast Asia. They spend most of their time resting on branches overhanging the water. If they sense danger, they quickly drop into the water many feet below.

▲ A water dragon resting on a branch above the water.

Crafty catfish

A shovel-nosed catfish spends the day hiding under the water plants. At night, it comes out and starts to look for food on the riverbed. It uses its long, whiskery snout to poke around in the mud for worms and small fish.

▲ Rainforest rivers provide plenty of food, but they can also be very dangerous places—especially when they flood after heavy rains.

▶ Catfish are often caught by rainforest people for food.

19

Amazon rainforest

The biggest rainforest on Earth grows along the banks of the Amazon River in South America. It covers an enormous 3.7 million square miles, which is almost the same size as Australia.

Ecuador
Amazon Rainforest
Brazil
South America

▼ Scarlet macaws.

▼ The mighty Amazon River snakes through the world's largest rainforest.

▲ The Amazon rainforest makes up more than half of all the rainforest territory left in the world.

Chatty macaws

Macaws are large, brightly colored parrots that live in the rainforest. They feed on nuts and seeds, cracking them open with their big, powerful beaks. Macaws often gather in flocks, calling, squawking, and screaming to keep in touch with each other.

Sleepy sloth

Sloths spend most of their lives hanging upside down from trees. This helps them to save energy. Their long, curved claws lock tightly around a branch so that they don't fall off, even when they are asleep.

▶ Sloths spend most of their lives asleep!

AWESOME!

One in ten of all known species of animals and plants lives in the Amazon rainforest. Incredibly, it is home to at least 2.5 million species of insects and 2,000 species of mammals and birds.

▶ One minute, the butterfly flashes bright blue...

▼ ...the next, it looks dull brown.

Blue butterfly

On top, a blue morpho butterfly's wings are bright blue and black. Underneath, they are brown with dark spots. As the butterfly flies through the forest, its wings flash blue, then brown—so that it appears, then disappears. This makes it difficult for birds and other predators to catch it.

Mammals

A huge range of mammals live in the rainforest, from tiny mice and rats to giant bats, apes, and even elephants and rhinoceroses. They have all adapted to life in the trees and on the ground.

▲ Mammals, such as these chorongo monkeys from Ecuador in South America, have many different ways of finding food—while also staying safe.

Pinecone pangolins

Pangolins spend the day in burrows, then come out at night to feed on termites. When danger threatens, the pangolin rolls itself into a hard, tight ball to protect its soft belly from attack.

◄ The pangolin's body is covered in sharp-edged scales that overlap like the tiles on a roof.

Sticky fingers

Aye ayes are odd-looking creatures from Madagascar, with a bushy tail, batlike ears, and huge, bright-orange eyes. They also have long, twiglike middle fingers for poking around under the bark of trees to search for juicy grubs.

◀ The aye aye finds grubs by listening for their movements.

Record rodents

Capybaras, the world's biggest rodents, look like giant guinea pigs. They live in large groups by rivers, where they feed on grass and water plants. They also eat their own droppings, which helps them to digest their food. With webbed feet for swimming, they are well adapted for life in the water.

▼ Capybaras are just as much at home in the water as they are on dry land.

Forest hunters

Many of the top predators in the rainforests are mammals, such as big cats. They hunt and kill other animals. To do this, they need sharp senses and killer features, such as sharp teeth and claws.

Jungle jaguar

Jaguars patrol the South American rainforests, looking for deer, tapirs, and wild pigs. Sometimes, they drop down onto their prey from trees. They are also excellent swimmers, catching caimans and capybaras.

▼ Jaguars have strong jaws and sharp teeth. They can kill their prey with a single bite.

AWESOME!

Sun bears live in Southeast Asian rainforests. They use their long, sharp claws and teeth to break open termite mounds to reach the insects inside. They also rip open tree trunks to reach wild bees.

Clouded leopard

Clouded leopards live in the rainforests of Southeast Asia, and are brilliant climbers. They can hang upside down from the branches and climb down tree trunks head first. These leopards also drag their food up into trees to eat it.

▶ At night, clouded leopards come down from the trees to hunt for deer, pigs, and monkeys.

Tiger stripes

A tiger's stripy coat hides it in the undergrowth as it hunts deer, cattle, and goats. It stalks its prey silently until it is within range. Then, it pounces. It brings its victim down with its huge front paws, then kills it with a lethal bite.

▼ ▲ Many big cats have markings that make them difficult to see. This means they can sneak up and pounce on their prey without being seen.

▶ Bengal tigers are found in India, China, Bangladesh, Indonesia, and other Southeast Asian countries.

On the move

Rainforest mammals have many ways of moving around to find food and escape from enemies. Some swing or climb through the trees. Some can fly or glide from branch to branch. Others are excellent swimmers.

◄ Gibbons live in small family groups in the treetops. They use long, loud calls to defend their territory from other gibbons.

Swinging gibbons

Gibbons are very fast, acrobatic apes. They swing from one branch to another, using their very long arms and strong, hook-shaped hands to hold on. Gibbons spend most of their lives in trees, and hardly ever go down to the ground.

Flying foxes

Flying foxes, or fruit bats, feed on fruit and flower nectar, which they find by smell. They fly through the forest and use their sharp, curved claws to grip onto trees. During the day, they rest in the treetops, dangling upside down.

▲ Flying foxes have huge, leathery wings that can measure more than 5ft across.

▼ River otters normally measure up to about 5ft long—but giant otters can reach 6ft.

Giant otters

Giant otters look clumsy on land but are strong, graceful swimmers. They use their large, webbed feet as paddles and their long tails to steer as they drift around in the water. These otters normally hunt for fish, but they also eat small caimans and snakes.

Tropical birds

Rainforest trees make perfect places for birds to find food, build nests, and raise their young. Birds also live on the forest floor, where they forage for insects and worms among the roots and leaves.

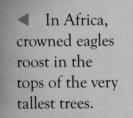

◀ In Africa, crowned eagles roost in the tops of the very tallest trees.

▲ Hoatzins are the size of chickens. They live in South America, in swampy areas around the Amazon and Orinoco rivers.

Eagle-eyed hunters

Crown eagles have powerful legs and long, sharp talons for killing monkeys, small antelopes, and mongooses. One of its favorite ways of hunting is to sit in a tree overlooking a waterhole, and then simply drop down onto its prey.

Pitta patter

Pittas are brightly colored birds that spend most of their time on the forest floor. They use their keen eyesight and sense of smell to find worms and snails to eat. Some smash the snail shells open on rocks and tree roots.

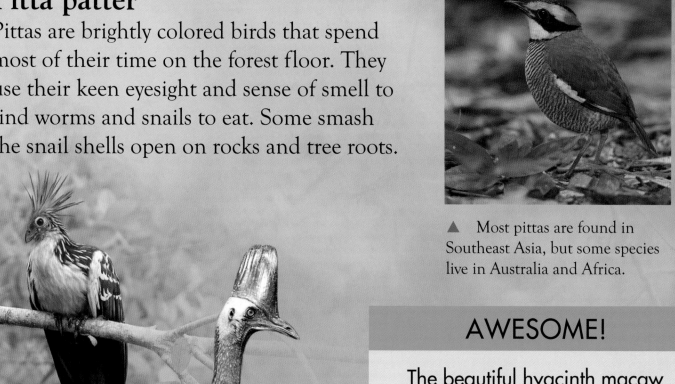

▲ Most pittas are found in Southeast Asia, but some species live in Australia and Africa.

AWESOME!

The beautiful hyacinth macaw is the world's largest parrot, measuring about 3ft from its head to the tip of its tail. It has blue feathers, a black beak, and patches of bright yellow skin on its face.

◄ The cassowary may use its helmet as a battering ram for crashing through the forest undergrowth.

Headstrong cassowary

Cassowaries are large, flightless birds that live in Australia and New Guinea. They stand around 6.5ft tall. On their heads, they have odd, bony helmets. No one is quite sure why.

Fruits and flowers

Many rainforest birds feed on leaves, fruits, buds, nuts, nectar, and pollen. Some of these birds have special features, such as an extra-strong or extra-long beak, to help them to tackle their favorite food.

Helpful hornbills

Rainforest plants need to spread out their seeds, and rely on birds and other animals to help them do this. Hornbills eat fruits and berries. As they fly, they pass droppings that contain lots of seeds from the food they've eaten.

▶ A macaw's beak is so strong that it can crack open rock-hard Brazil nuts.

◀ Hornbills use their large beaks to catch food, build nests, clean their feathers—and fight.

Hover birds

Hummingbirds hover in front of flowers to feed on their sugary nectar. As the birds feed, they get covered in pollen, which they then carry to other flowers, allowing new seeds to grow.

▲ The hummingbird's long, thin beak is specially adapted to get deep into the flower.

Nut crackers

Macaws eat all sorts of nuts and seeds, which they break open with their sharp, curved beaks. They also nibble at riverbank clay to get the essential salts and minerals that their body needs.

AWESOME!

Hanging parrots from Asia hang upside down from branches. From a distance, they look like bunches of leaves—so their enemies leave them alone.

Finding a mate

Male birds look for a female mate who can lay eggs that will hatch into young. Some make dancelike movements or show off their fabulous feathers, hoping that a female will pick them out. Others build shelters or use loud voices to call to females.

Say it with sticks

Male satin bowerbirds build amazing stick shelters, called bowers, on the forest floor. They decorate them with shiny blue berries, fruits, and flowers to attract a female. The females visit different bowers and choose the male with the best one.

▼ This male bowerbird has also collected artificial blue objects as gifts to attract a mate.

▼ Most birds of paradise come from New Guinea.

Birds of paradise

Birds of paradise live up to their name. The females are dull in color—but the males have a spectacular plumage. The Count Raggi's bird of paradise fans and shakes its feathers to show off to females, sometimes hanging upside down from a branch.

Pheasant feathers

A male great argus pheasant of Southeast Asia has very long tail and wing feathers. Once it has cleared a space on the forest floor, the male bird fans out its wings and "dances" to show off its patterns.

▲ The pheasant's wing feathers are decorated with rows of large markings that look like eyes.

▶ The great argus pheasant can grow to 6.5ft in length.

Asian rainforests

In Asia, there are patches of rainforest in India and the countries of the southeast. Some of these tropical forests grow on the mainland, and some grow on scattered islands such as Borneo.

Nosey monkeys

Male proboscis monkeys from Borneo are famous for their big, bulging noses. Amazingly, these outsized noses help the monkeys to attract mates. A male uses his nose like a loudspeaker to boost the sound of his call—and impress a female.

▲ Many amazing and unusual animals live in the rainforests of India and Southeast Asia.

▼ The nose of a male proboscis monkey can grow to more than four inches long.

Night vision

Tarsiers are very small creatures, with enormous eyes for spotting their prey of insects at night. They also have very long back legs and toes for climbing, clinging, and leaping through trees.

AWESOME!

The Atlas moth is the biggest moth in the world. Its wings have maplike patterns on them and measure about 12 inches across—that's wider than your outstretched hands.

▲ Each eye is the same size and weight as the tarsier's brain.

Catlike killers

Green cat snakes live among the trees overhanging the water, where their coloring makes them hard to see. At night, they hunt lizards and frogs. They inject their prey with venom, then swallow it whole.

► Green cat snakes have large, catlike eyes—adapted for seeing well at night.

Reptiles

Rainforest reptiles range from tiny, dwarf chameleons to enormous crocodiles and alligators. They can climb, swim, and slither, and are found all over the forest, from the tall trees of the canopy to rivers and streams.

▼ Crocodiles have their eyes and nostrils on top of their heads, so that they can still see and breathe while in the water.

▼ Chameleons usually have green or brown markings to blend in with the rainforest trees.

Chameleon colors

Chameleons are extraordinary creatures that can change color, often to communicate and show what sort of mood they are in. If an intruder enters its territory, a chameleon will turn much darker in color—to show an increase in fear and aggression.

Crunching caiman

Caimans are related to alligators and crocodiles. The biggest is the black caiman, which can grow up to 15ft long. It lurks in the water, waiting for prey to pass by, then it snaps them up with its sharp, pointed teeth.

▲ Black caimans live in slow-moving rivers and streams in South America.

Walking on water

The basilisk lizard from Central America has an unusual way of escaping from its enemies. It jumps into the river and races across the surface, without falling in. When the danger is over, the lizard swims for the shore.

▲ To stop it from sinking, the lizard slaps at the water with its long legs, big feet, and long, wide toes.

AWESOME!

A chameleon can swivel each of its bulging, cone-shaped eyes separately. This helps it to look all around its body. When it sees prey, it focuses both eyes in the same direction.

Snakes of the rainforest

Rainforests make brilliant homes for slithering snakes of all kinds. Snakes need warmth to stay active, but they also need shady places to avoid too much sunshine. There is also plenty of prey to feed on in rainforests—rodents, frogs, birds, and insects.

▼ The eyelash viper is venomous, and can strike at its prey with lightning speed.

Ssssupersized

Anacondas are enormous, reaching 26ft in length and weighing more than 500lbs. They can eat animals as large as deer, by wrapping their bodies around them and squeezing them to death.

Eyelash vipers

The beautiful but deadly eyelash viper gets its name from the bristly scales above its eyes. These scales may have adapted in this way to break up the shape of the snake's body as it hides among the leaves.

◄ Anacondas are superb swimmers. They spend most of their time in the water, lying in wait for their prey.

Flying snake

In Southeast Asia, some snakes can glide through the air. First, they slither to the end of a branch and dangle in a J-shape. Then they take off. They can "fly" up to 165ft from one tree to another.

▼ Flying snakes don't have wings. They flatten out their bodies to catch the air.

AWESOME!

The gaboon viper from Africa has the longest fangs of any snake. They are an awesome two inches long—that's about as long as your little finger.

Insects

There are more types of insects in the rainforest than any other kind of animal. There are at least one million species—and there may be millions more, waiting to be discovered. They include tiny ants, giant beetles, huge butterflies, and cleverly camouflaged stick insects.

Cutting edge

Leaf-cutter ants are tiny, but they are also incredibly strong. Each ant can carry a piece of leaf weighing around 50 times its own weight. They collect the leaves to make gardens in their nests, where they grow a special fungus. The fungus is their food.

AWESOME!

Paper wasps are master builders. They create umbrella-shaped nests high up in the trees. They make the "paper" for their nests from dead wood and plant stems, which they chew up and mix with their spit.

◀ Leaf-cutter ants snip the leaves with their sharp jaws, and then carry the pieces back to their nests.

Jungle giraffe

This little weevil from Madagascar is one of the oddest-looking insects in the rainforest. The male is about one inch long, with a giraffe-like head and neck about half as long as the rest of its body. No one is exactly sure what this extra-long neck is for.

▶ A male weevil could possibly use its neck to fight with rivals to win a female mate.

▼ This Richmond birdwing butterfly, of Australia, is large—but it is only about half the size of the Queen Alexandra birdwing.

Record-breaker

Birdwing butterflies are very large. The Queen Alexandra birdwing lives in a small patch of rainforest in Papua New Guinea. With a wingspan of 11 inches, it is the biggest butterfly in the world. Red hairs on its body warn hungry enemies that it is venomous.

Masters of disguise

Many rainforest insects use colors and patterns to hide from hungry predators. Some also disguise themselves to catch their prey by surprise, while others pretend to be more dangerous than they really are.

Double trouble

A false leaf katydid looks just like a dead, brown leaf on the forest floor. If this disguise does not work, it has another trick. Quick as a flash, it can flick its wings open to show off its eyespots. This startles a predator long enough for the insect to escape.

▶ Over time, the colors of this mantis have adapted to look like those of an orchid's flowers.

◀ This katydid's wings look just like leaves, right down to the tiny veins.

Perfect petals

The orchid mantis has the perfect disguise. Its body is the same color as the orchid flower it rests on—even its legs and wings look like petals. The mantis stays still, waiting for small insects to pass by.

▼ The mantis grabs insects with its front legs, then gobbles them up.

AWESOME!

Some rainforest moths—such as this comet moth from Madagascar—have large, eyelike markings on their wings. These may frighten enemies away, or trick them into leaving the moth's real head alone.

▼ Just like real sticks, stick insects are sometimes covered in lichen or moss.

Giant walking stick

Some rainforest stick insects can grow as long as your arm—but they are extremely difficult to spot. Many have a long, thin, brown body and look exactly like a stick. Some also pretend to be dead, if they are attacked.

Food and feeding

Insects make tasty snacks for lots of rainforest animals. But the forest also supplies insects with plenty of food to eat. Some insects feed on leaves and flowers. Others eat each other!

▲ Driver ants travel in enormous swarms, many millions strong.

Praying mantis

The praying mantis is a fearsome predator. It snatches moths, crickets, grasshoppers, and flies by shooting out its long front legs. These mantises also feed on each other—females sometimes even eat their mates!

▼ The mantis's legs have sharp spikes on them for pinning down their prey.

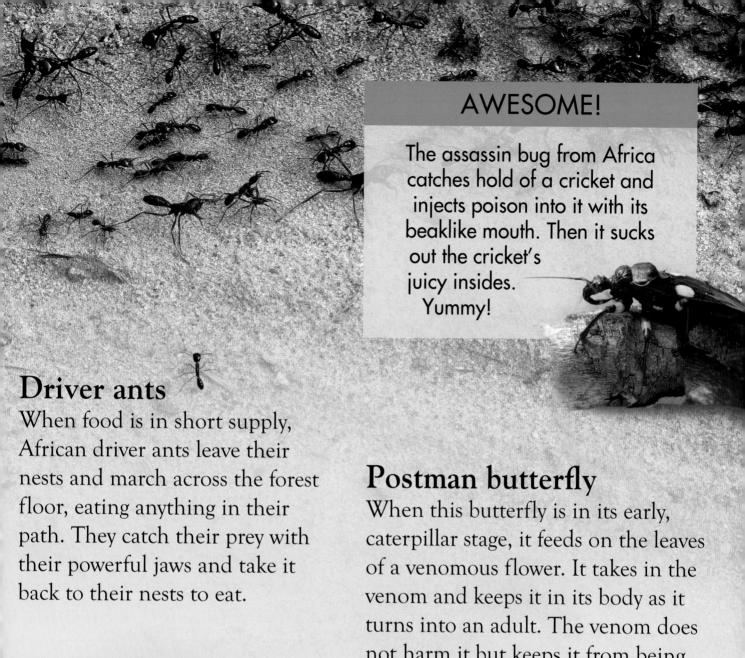

The assassin bug from Africa catches hold of a cricket and injects poison into it with its beaklike mouth. Then it sucks out the cricket's juicy insides. Yummy!

Driver ants

When food is in short supply, African driver ants leave their nests and march across the forest floor, eating anything in their path. They catch their prey with their powerful jaws and take it back to their nests to eat.

Postman butterfly

When this butterfly is in its early, caterpillar stage, it feeds on the leaves of a venomous flower. It takes in the venom and keeps it in its body as it turns into an adult. The venom does not harm it but keeps it from being eaten by predators.

▶ This insect was named the postman butterfly because it follows the same path from flower to flower every day.

African rainforests

Rainforests grow in West and Central Africa, mostly along the banks of the River Congo. The Congo rainforest is the second largest in the world, after the mighty Amazon of South America.

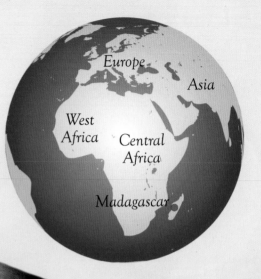

Europe

Asia

West Africa

Central Africa

Madagascar

▲ There are also small patches of rainforest on the island of Madagascar, off the east coast of Africa.

◄ Okapis have big ears and a dark, velvety coat with stripes on their backside and legs.

The shy okapi

The okapi is a timid and secretive animal, related to the giraffe. It grazes on rainforest trees and shrubs, pulling off the leaves with its long tongue.

▶ Chimpanzees live in large family groups in the rainforests of Central and West Africa.

Sleepy chimps

Chimpanzees feed on fruit, leaves, and insects, but also work together to hunt larger animals, such as colobus monkeys. At night, the adults build leafy nests in the treetops where they and their young can sleep, safe from night-time predators.

AWESOME!

The giant African millipede has around 256 legs and grows up to 15 inches long—that's about the length from your elbow to your fingertips. When it is threatened, it curls up into a tight ball on the forest floor.

Elephant shrews

Elephant shrews, or sengis, are not actually shrews—they are related to elephants. They have a long, bendy snout that can twist and turn in search of food, just like an elephant's trunk.

▶ Sengis are small and furry with a scaly tail and long legs, which they use for hopping around.

Amphibians

Amphibians live all over the rainforest. They range from frogs and toads to salamanders and caecilians. Some live high in the canopy to avoid hungry predators. Others are superbly disguised on the forest floor.

▼ The marine toad, or cane toad, can weigh a whopping two kilograms!

Greedy guts

The marine toad is found along the banks of the Amazon River. It eats anything it can fit into its mouth, including large insects, small snakes, lizards, and mice. It will even eat bees straight out of their hive—and its own young, if it is very hungry.

AWESOME!

Tomato frogs from Madagascar have sneaky ways of protecting themselves. They puff up their body, then ooze out a sticky glue from their skin, which gums up an attacker's eyes and mouth.

Rubbery eels

Rubber eels are from a group of amphibians called caecilians. They spend a lot of their time burrowing underground, but they are also good swimmers. Caecilians are nearly blind and find their food—of insects and earthworms—mostly by taste and smell.

▶ Leaflike skin texture.

Frogs in disguise

With its blotchy brown markings, the long-nosed horned frog of Southeast Asia looks just like a dry, dead leaf. Its skin has folds that look like leaf veins, and it has spiky horns on its head that break up its frog shape. Tree frogs, such as the one below, are also very well camouflaged.

▲ Until this frog moves, it is almost impossible to see against the forest floor!

▼ This beautiful peacock tree frog is from Tanzania, in Africa.

49

Fabulous frogs

The most common amphibians living in the rainforest are frogs. There are many different kinds—some tiny, some huge, some brightly colored, some well hidden. Others are venomous, while some appear to fly.

Beware: poison!

The poison dart frog's brightly colored skin is a message to its enemies. It warns others that this tiny frog is dangerous to eat. Its skin contains a venom so strong that a single drop can kill a monkey in just a few seconds.

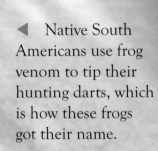

◀ Native South Americans use frog venom to tip their hunting darts, which is how these frogs got their name.

Flying frogs

In the rainforests of Southeast Asia, there are frogs that can glide from branch to branch. To escape from predators, they stretch out the webs of skin between their long fingers and toes, then launch themselves from a tree, like little parachutes.

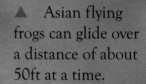

▲ Asian flying frogs can glide over a distance of about 50ft at a time.

◀ By night, most tree frogs hunt for insects. By day, they hide in cracks and holes.

Tree frogs

Tree frogs are brilliant climbers. They have round, sticky pads on their fingers and toes to help them cling onto leaves and tree bark. The skin on their bellies, which is loose and sticky, also helps them to grip the trees.

AWESOME!

The gigantic goliath frog from Africa is the biggest frog in the world. It can grow to more than 12 inches in length. It lives near rivers, where it feeds mostly on water plants.

Fish

The rivers and streams that run through the rainforests are home to a wide variety of fish. In the Amazon River alone, there are around 5,000 different fish species. Often, even small pools and puddles are full of life.

Peckish piranhas

Armed with rows of razor-sharp teeth, piranhas swim and hunt in large groups. By hunting together, they can tackle animals much larger than themselves, such as caimans, manatees, and anacondas. Some piranhas are vegetarians, feeding on fruit and seeds.

▲ Piranhas have such sharp teeth that local people sometimes use them as scissors or knives.

Piracucu

The piracucu, or arapaima, is a huge fish that lives in the Amazon River. It can reach 6.5ft in length and weigh up to 440lbs. It feeds on fish, shellfish, and even small land animals.

▲ The piracucu is a torpedo-shaped fish with dark green scales and red markings.

Rainforest fishing

The fire-mouth panchax gets its name from the male's red throat. These fish live in small pools of water that fill up in the wet season. They feed on insects and grow quickly, laying lots of eggs. When the dry season comes, the pools dry up and the fish die, but their eggs are left behind in the mud and hatch as soon as it rains again.

AWESOME!

Electric eels feed mainly on other fish. They give off strong electric shocks to stun their prey and warn off predators.

▶ Local rainforest people hunt fish, such as the piracucu, for their meat. Traditionally, they catch the fish with nets and spears, or with bows and arrows.

53

Rainforest spiders

Thousands of different kinds of spiders live in the rainforests. Some are tiny; others are as big as plates. Some spin huge webs to catch their prey; others hunt for food on the forest floor.

Super spider

The goliath bird-eating spider from South America is the biggest spider in the world (by weight). It lives on the forest floor and comes out at night to hunt. It lies in wait, then pounces and bites into its victim with its venomous fangs.

Spinning tales

Orb weaver spiders spin webs as big as bed sheets between the rainforest trees. Then the female sits in front of the web, waiting for prey. The webs are big enough to catch animals as large as frogs and hummingbirds.

◀ Including its long, hairy legs, the goliath spider can grow as large as a dinner plate.

▶ This jumping spider is sitting near a flower, waiting to pounce.

◀ Orb weaver webs are so strong that rainforest people can use them to make fishing nets.

Sneaky spiders

Jumping spiders feed on smaller spiders. They will sit on a spider's web, looking like a trapped insect. They might even pluck on the web to make it vibrate, as if they are stuck and struggling. When the web's owner comes to investigate, the jumping spider pounces.

AWESOME!

The Brazilian wandering spider is one of the world's most venomous spiders. When it is threatened, it lifts up its front legs and shows off its deadly fangs.

More creepy-crawlies

Spiders are not the only creepy-crawlies at home in the rainforests. There are hundreds of other animals—including scorpions, millipedes, centipedes, leeches, and snails—hiding among the trees and on the forest floor.

AWESOME!

Apple snails live in rivers but lay their eggs on the trunks of trees. This keeps them safe from hungry fish. When the baby snails hatch, they drop straight into the water below.

Bloodsuckers

Leeches feed on the blood of other animals. They sink their sharp teeth into a victim, then hang on tight. When full, they drop off. A leech can suck up 15 times its own weight in blood in just one meal.

◀ Once a leech has filled up with blood, it does not need to eat for another six months or so.

Giant in a small world

The Amazonian giant centipede is big and fierce enough to hunt animals such as insects, large spiders, lizards, frogs, and snakes. It uses a pair of sharp claws to tear into its prey and inject it with venom.

◄ This giant centipede's bright colors warn its enemies that it is venomous.

Sting in the tail

The gigantic emperor scorpion has a glossy, black body, large pinchers, and a long, curled tail with a deadly sting at the end. The scorpion uses its sting in self-defense and for catching insect prey. It hunts at night, using hairs on its body to sense the whereabouts of its prey.

▲ Adult scorpions can grow up to eight inches long and can weigh one ounce.

Australasian rainforests

In Australia, there are three small patches of rainforest along the northeastern coast. They are all that is left of a much bigger, ancient forest. To the north lies the island of New Guinea, which still has large areas of rainforest.

Southeast Asia

New Guinea

Queensland

Australia

▶ The Blyth's hornbill is famous for its big, bony beak. It lives in the rainforests of Papua New Guinea.

◀ Some of the rainforest in New Guinea has yet to be explored by people.

Duck-billed burrower

Duck-billed platypuses live in rivers and streams, where they use their ducklike bills to scoop up worms, insects, and shellfish from the riverbed. They dig burrows, with underwater entrances, along the riverbank.

◀ Platypuses store food in their cheeks, then rise to the surface to chew and swallow it.

Security conscious

For safety, the female Blyth's hornbill builds her nest inside a hollow tree trunk, then seals herself in behind a wall of mud. There is a small slit for the male to pass through food. She stays there for several weeks, until her chicks are ready to leave the nest.

▶ Ghost bats are named after their very thin, ghostly looking wings.

Flying phantoms

Deathly pale ghost bats fly silently through the Australian rainforest at night. They find their prey—of mice, lizards ,and insects—using echolocation. Then they pin it down with their sharp claws and kill it with a bite to the neck.

AWESOME!

Over the last 20 years, more than 1,000 new kinds of animals and plants have been found in the rainforests of New Guinea.

Animals in danger

Every day, huge areas of rainforest are destroyed. Trees are cut down for their timber or burnt to make space for farms, mines, and new roads. This has a devastating effect on animals, who are left with nowhere to live or find food. Many of them are in danger of becoming extinct.

Rare rhinos

Sumatran rhinos are the smallest type of rhino. They once roamed across large parts of Asia, but today only a few hundred survive. Their close relative, the Javan rhino, may already be extinct.

▼ Sumatran rhinos now live in small patches of forest on the islands of Sumatra and Borneo.

NOT SO AWESOME!

No one has seen a Spix's macaw in the wild for more than 13 years. There are, however, about 100 of these macaws living in zoos and wildlife parks.

◀ The Amazon manatee lives in the Amazon River, where it feeds on water plants.

Disappearing manatees

Large herds of Amazon manatees were once found, but so many have been killed for their meat and fat that they are now very rare. The destruction of the forest around them means they also have a lot less food to eat.

▶ Lowland gorillas feed mostly on fruit—around 100 different kinds have been found in their diet.

Lowland losses

Lowland gorillas live in the rainforests of Central Africa. Huge parts of these forests have been cut down for timber. The gorillas are also hunted for their meat, and for body parts used in traditional medicine.

▶ On the islands of Borneo and Sumatra, in Southeast Asia, orangutans are under serious threat.

Saving the animals

Around the world, people are working hard to save the rainforests and their wildlife. Some patches of forest are being set aside as parks, and new forests are being planted. Conservationists are also teaching people and businesses how to use the forests without damaging them.

Success story

In the 1980s, only 200 golden lion tamarins were left. Luckily, government and conservation groups took action to protect their habitat. Also, 140 zoos around the world began to breed tamarins in captivity, returning them to the wild when they are ready.

◀ Golden lion tamarins come from the rainforests of Brazil in South America.

Threatening fungus

Many kinds of rainforest frogs are being wiped out by a deadly fungus. Biologists in places such as Panama are trying to save them. They collect the frogs and transport them to special containers in zoos, where they can keep them alive and safe.

Rescuing orangutans

Some organizations adopt homeless orangutans and look after them until they can be released back into the wild, in specially protected patches of forest. Others try to stop orangutans from being caught and sold as pets.

▶ This lemur tree frog lives in Costa Rica, Panama, and Colombia.

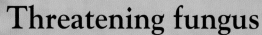

NOT SO AWESOME!

Today, there are only about 40,000 orangutans left in Borneo, and around 7,500 in Sumatra. If we don't protect them, there may be none left in ten years' time.

Ocean life

Oceans cover almost three quarters of our planet. These watery worlds are filled with an amazing variety of living things. Many creatures are only found in the sea, such as octopuses, jellyfish, and giant tube worms. There are also fish, shellfish, birds, mammals, sea snakes, seaweeds, and even ocean insects.

▲ The polar bear is the only ocean bear. It spends some of its time on land, but is also brilliant at swimming underwater.

What is an ocean?

The word "ocean" usually means a huge, salty sea covering a large area of the Earth. There are five main oceans. The biggest are the Pacific, Atlantic, and Indian oceans. The Arctic and Antarctic (or Southern) oceans are at the top and bottom of the world.

▼ Jellyfish are strange-looking sea creatures. They are often partly see-through, with long, trailing tentacles.

Seas and oceans

Seas are really no different from oceans—they are just smaller. The Red Sea, for example, is a narrow sea lying between Africa and Arabia. Seas can be part of larger oceans—such as the Caribbean Sea, which is in the Atlantic Ocean.

▲ The world's main seas and oceans are all joined together, as you can see on this map.

▼ Fierce, scary-looking viperfish are found in deep oceans.

Wide and deep

One reason there are so many sea creatures is that the oceans are truly huge. They are also very deep. Different types of creatures live at different levels, from the sunny shallows to the dark and gloomy depths.

◄ The Portuguese man-of-war is a bizarre, jellyfish-like animal. It uses its inflatable sail to float along on the sea's surface.

AWESOME!

Oceans are so big and deep that there may be many sea creatures still waiting to be discovered. Scientists often find new ones, such as octopuses, sharks, and strange, deep-sea fish.

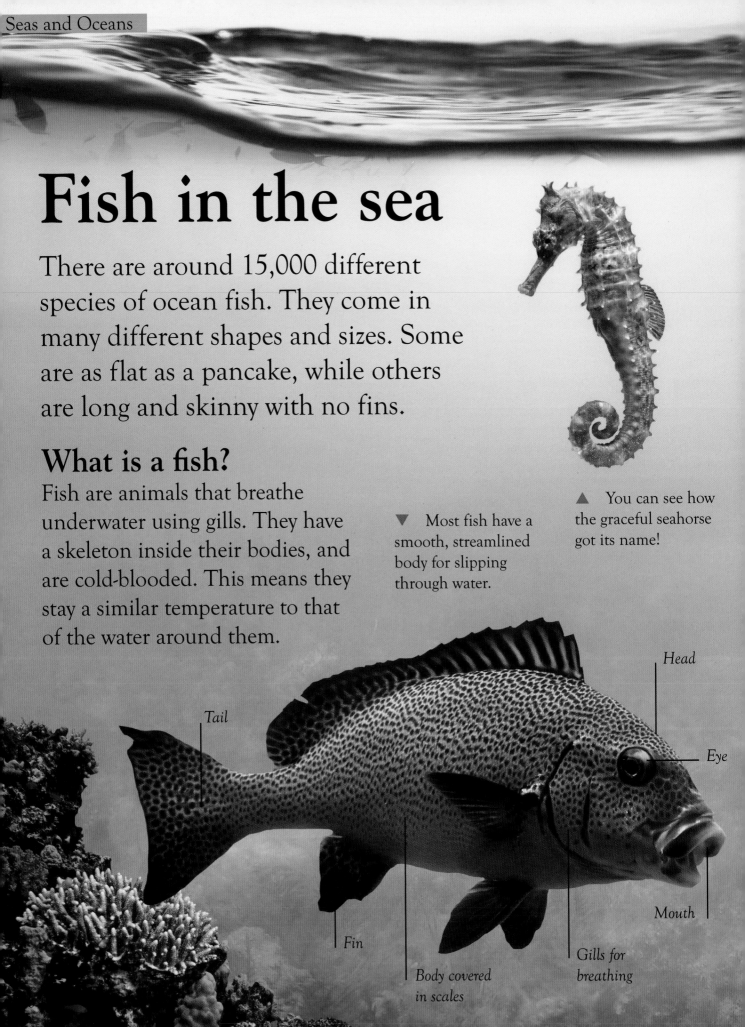

Fish in the sea

There are around 15,000 different species of ocean fish. They come in many different shapes and sizes. Some are as flat as a pancake, while others are long and skinny with no fins.

What is a fish?

Fish are animals that breathe underwater using gills. They have a skeleton inside their bodies, and are cold-blooded. This means they stay a similar temperature to that of the water around them.

▼ Most fish have a smooth, streamlined body for slipping through water.

▲ You can see how the graceful seahorse got its name!

Head

Eye

Tail

Mouth

Fin

Gills for breathing

Body covered in scales

▲ Flying fish
really do fly!

Sharks and rays

Sharks and rays are fish, too. Unlike most fish, they don't have scales—they have tough skin instead. Their skeletons are made of bendy cartilage, not bone. They eat fish, dolphins, seals, squid, shellfish, and plankton.

▲ Most fish lay eggs, but not all sharks do. Some, like the blue shark, give birth to live babies.

▼ Copperband butterflyfish use their long snout to feed on coral, shrimp, and anemones.

Fish food

Different types of fish eat different foods. Some are seaweed-nibblers, while others are fierce hunters. Some eat tiny ocean plants and animals called plankton. Some feed on coral, dead animals, and even on other fish.

▲ A shoal of sardines
darting and changing direction
to avoid a hungry lionfish.

▶ Rays have a flat body
with wide, winglike fins.

Minnows and monsters

Ocean fish range from tiny
gobies, smaller than a grape, to
enormous sharks as big as a bus.
Some fish are so massive that
they've been known to flatten
whole boats when they leap out
of the sea and crash back down.

Swimming in shoals

Smaller fish often stick
together in big groups, called
shoals or schools. Sardines
live in shoals of thousands
or even millions of fish!
Being in a group means
fish can work together to
watch out for danger.

Filter feeders

Some of the biggest fish of all eat the smallest prey. The whale shark, the largest fish in the sea, moves along slowly, sucking in lots of water. Then it filters plankton and small fish from the water and swallows them.

▲ Whale sharks are huge—up to 40ft long—but they are quite gentle.

Ocean giants

Besides enormous sharks and rays, two of the biggest fish in the oceans are the odd-looking sunfish and the giant oarfish.

▲ The ocean sunfish can grow to be 10ft long and 13ft from fin to fin, and can weigh more than a car.

▶ A sailfish can raise and lower the fin on its back, like a boat's sail.

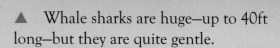

AWESOME!

Stout infantfish are the smallest fish—adult males are about a quarter of an inch long.

Sailfish are the fastest fish, reaching speeds of more than 60 miles per hour.

The deep-sea hagfish is the slimiest. It releases vast amounts of thick, snotty slime!

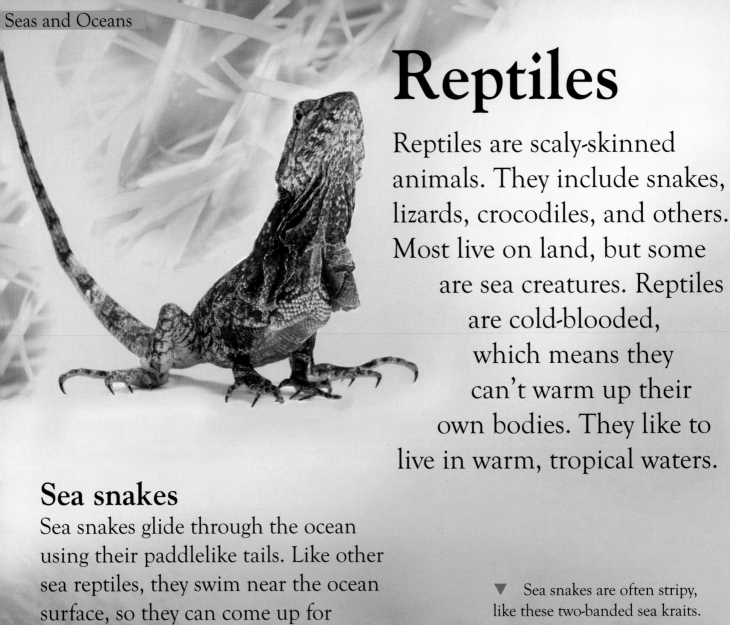

Reptiles

Reptiles are scaly-skinned animals. They include snakes, lizards, crocodiles, and others. Most live on land, but some are sea creatures. Reptiles are cold-blooded, which means they can't warm up their own bodies. They like to live in warm, tropical waters.

Sea snakes

Sea snakes glide through the ocean using their paddlelike tails. Like other sea reptiles, they swim near the ocean surface, so they can come up for air when they need to. Some sea snakes have a deadly, venomous bite.

▼ Sea snakes are often stripy, like these two-banded sea kraits.

Turtles

Sea turtles have a shell on their back and flippers for swimming. Some are huge—the leatherback turtle's shell can be up to 6.5ft long! Turtles mostly live in the sea, but lay their eggs on the shore.

◄ After mating, the female crawls up onto a sandy beach. She uses her back flippers to dig a nest in the sand.

▲ Green sea turtles swim long distances to their breeding areas to find a mate.

► She lays more than 100 eggs in the hole and covers them over with sand.

▲ After 50-60 days, the baby turtles hatch, dig themselves out, and crawl down to the sea.

Ocean-going crocs

American and saltwater crocodiles can live in the sea, as well as in rivers and swamps. The saltwater croc can grow to 23ft long. It's the world's biggest reptile.

AWESOME!

There is just one sea lizard—the marine iguana. It lies on rocky beaches to warm up in the sun, then dives into the sea to nibble on seaweed.

Ocean mammals

Most mammals live on land, but a few have adapted to life in the ocean. They still need to breathe air, but some can hold their breath for up to an hour to go on deep ocean dives.

Whales and dolphins

Whales and dolphins have smooth skin and streamlined, fish-shaped bodies. Instead of nostrils, they have a blowhole on top of their head, to make it easier to breathe while swimming.

▼ How can you tell a dolphin from a shark?

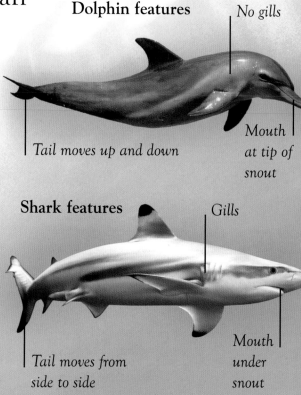

Dolphin features

No gills

Tail moves up and down

Mouth at tip of snout

Shark features

Gills

Tail moves from side to side

Mouth under snout

◀ Seals are fast and nimble in the water—but on land, they have to flop and wriggle around.

The seal family

Seals, sea lions, and walruses are furry sea mammals. They are all hunters, feeding on fish, shellfish, crabs, seabirds, or squid. A thick layer of fatty blubber, under their skin, helps to keep them warm.

Polar bears

Polar bears have thick, white fur to blend in with ice and snow, and big front paws for swimming. Polar bears swim long distances to find seals to hunt for food.

▲ Polar bear cubs have a close bond with their mom. They feed on her nutritious milk.

The strange sirenians

Manatees and dugongs are large, slow-moving sea mammals that live in warm, shallow seas. They like to wander around, snooze, and graze on seagrasses that grow on the shallow seabed.

◀ Dugongs and manatees are often called sea cows—because of the way they hoover up seagrass.

▶ When an orca jumps, its whole body comes out of the water—and then smashes down again.

AWESOME!

Scientists have found that some sea mammals are very clever. For example, orcas (killer whales) make waves to wash seals off the ice so they can catch them.

Birds of the sea

On a trip to the seaside, you might hear the squawks and cries of the seagulls, terns, puffins, or penguins that live there. Seabirds often nest in huge groups, called colonies, on sea ice or cliffs, and hunt for food in the ocean.

▲ The wandering albatross is the biggest species, with a wingspan of 10–13ft.

Penguins

Penguins can't fly, as they have flippers instead of wings. They use them for swerving and steering underwater, chasing fish, and avoiding hunters, such as leopard seals. Penguins live in the southern hemisphere of the world, including the freezing-cold continent of Antarctica.

The soaring albatross

Albatrosses are enormous, swooping seabirds that glide huge distances across the ocean. They can spend up to ten years out at sea, only returning to land when they are ready to nest and have chicks.

▼ Penguins leap into the water to feed. They get back onto land or ice by launching themselves up to 6.5ft into the air.

Gannets (below) catch fish by folding up their wings—forming a rocket shape—and plunging into the sea at speeds of up to 75 miles per hour.

Nesting in numbers

Seagulls and their relatives—skuas, petrels, puffins, and gannets—are the most common seabirds. Their huge nesting colonies can completely cover a craggy cliff or island, turning it white with seabirds and droppings.

▼ This is a puffin nesting colony on Farne Island, off the northeast coast of England.

◄ Adult puffins take it in turns to keep their eggs warm and to feed their young.

75

Molluscs

The mollusc family includes snails, shellfish, octopuses, and squid. There are more mollusc species than fish species in the sea, and they make up a quarter of all types of sea creatures.

Seashells

The creatures that live in seashells are mainly molluscs. If a shell has two matching parts, held together with a hinge, it's a bivalve mollusc—such as an oyster, mussel, or scallop. Bivalves feed on tiny bits of food in the water. Some anchor themselves to rocks, while others, such as scallops, can swim by flapping their shells.

▼ Giant clams can grow to more than three feet across.

▼ Nudibranchs have stinging cells, similar to those of jellyfish.

Sea snails

A spiral-shaped or cone-shaped shell probably belongs to a sea snail. Sea snails usually have thicker, stronger shells than land snails, helping to protect them from predators such as crabs. Many use a sharp tongue to scrape algae off rocks.

Sea slugs

Sea slugs are like land slugs—they are related to snails, but don't have shells and so need other ways to protect themselves. They often have bright, vivid colors and patterns to warn hunters that they are venomous or taste revolting. Some can squirt acid and others have a venomous sting.

▶ Sea snails eat soft foods, such as marine plants and algae.

Octopuses and squid

The mollusc family also includes cephalopods, such as octopuses, cuttlefish, and squid. The name cephalopod means "head-foot," as their many legs (actually called arms) are attached to their heads.

Amazing octopuses

Octopuses have an astonishing ability to change not just their color, but their shape and texture, too. In seconds, a common octopus (right) can switch from smooth and white to looking like a bunch of brown, speckled, frilly seaweed.

Eye

Head

Mantle—the main body area

Arms with suckers for holding prey

A "siphon" squirts water to push the creature along.

▲ Parts of a common octopus.

◄ A blue-ringed octopus can blend in with its surroundings, then suddenly flash its bright, electric-blue ring markings.

Cuttlefish

Cuttlefish are not fish, but molluscs with eight short arms and two longer tentacles. They can send signals to each other by flashing quick-changing colors and patterns across their skin.

The nautilus (above) is the only type of modern cephalopod that has a shell. But in prehistoric times there were huge, octopuslike creatures with shells, called ammonites (below).

▲ Cephalopods, such as this cuttlefish, are relatives of slugs and snails. They do not have any bones.

Squid

Squid come in a huge range of sizes. The smallest is the pygmy squid—it's no bigger than your little finger! The biggest squid, the giant and colossal squid, can reach around 46ft long.

▶ These Caribbean coral reef squid are looking for prawns, crustaceans, and fish to feed on.

Crustaceans

Crustaceans, such as crabs, lobsters, and prawns, are very common. They get their name from their "crust"— their hard shell. They are related to insects and spiders. Like them, they have an "exoskeleton"—a skeleton on the outside of the body.

▲   People sometimes catch and eat isopods.

Crabs, lobsters, and prawns

These crustaceans all have ten legs. The front legs often have large claws or pincers for holding onto food. Most of these animals are scavengers, meaning they eat whatever they can find.

Giant isopod

This many-legged, creepy-crawly crustacean looks a bit like a pale pink woodlouse. It is related to the woodlouse, but it is much bigger—up to 16 inches long—and it lives on the deep seabed.

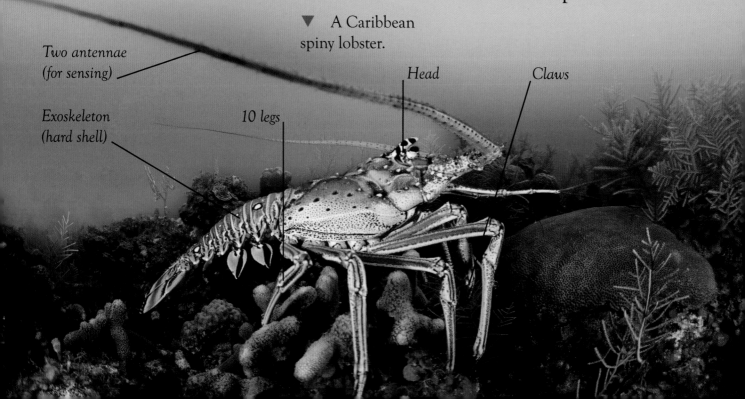

▼   A Caribbean spiny lobster.

Two antennae (for sensing)

Exoskeleton (hard shell)

10 legs

Head

Claws

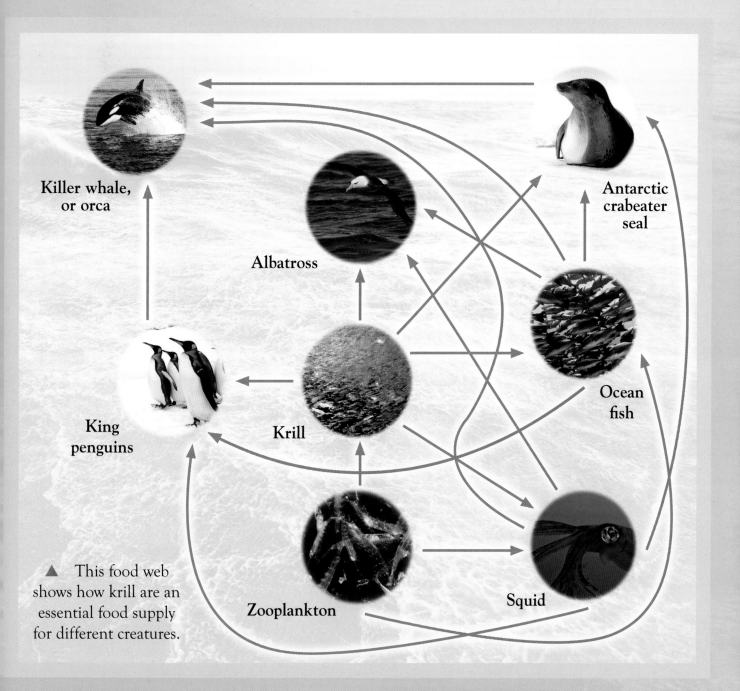

Killer whale, or orca

Albatross

Antarctic crabeater seal

King penguins

Krill

Ocean fish

Zooplankton

Squid

▲ This food web shows how krill are an essential food supply for different creatures.

Krillions!

Krill are small, pinkish crustaceans, similar to shrimp. There are trillions of them—so many that, if all of them were put together, they would weigh more than all the humans on Earth! They are very important, because many other sea creatures rely on them for food.

AWESOME!

The tiny snapping shrimp, just 1.5 inches long, makes one of the loudest sounds in the sea. When it snaps its claw shut, it creates a super-powerful sound wave, strong enough to break glass.

◀ Crown-of-thorns starfish usually have around 20 arms.

Starfish and sea urchins

Starfish and sea urchins belong to a bizarre family of sea creatures called echinoderms. Their name means "spiny skin" and they all have spines, prickles, or bumps.

Many-pointed stars

Most starfish have five arms, though they can have more. Starfish are hunters, and eat shellfish, crabs, and sea worms. There are around 1,500 different species of starfish, and some can have as many as 40 arms!

▲ Starfish move around using rows and rows of tiny, tubelike feet.

Hunting and feeding

A starfish eats its prey by holding it tight, then pushing its stomach out of its mouth and into its prey. The stomach digests the meal and turns it to liquid, which the starfish can then suck back into its body.

AWESOME!

If a starfish loses an arm, it can grow a new one to replace it. Not only that—the cut-off arm can sometimes grow into a whole new starfish!

Sea cucumbers

Like other echinoderms, the soft, sausage-shaped sea cucumber has five sections. The mouth is at one end, and five rows of tiny feet run along the body. Sea cucumbers eat bits of old food and other animals' poo.

▼ The skin of a sea cucumber feels a bit like leather.

Sea urchins

Sea urchins are round or oval, with a hard, spiny shell made up of ten sections. The urchin sticks its mouth out of a hole at the bottom to feed on algae.

▼ These Diadema sea urchins have very long, dark spines.

Jellyfish and sea anemones

Jellyfish, or jellies, are very strange animals. They have no brains, though some do have nerves that can detect movement and light. Some jellies are deadly.

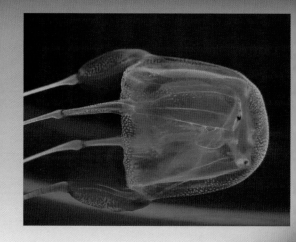

▲ The box jellyfish is almost see-through. It has a seriously deadly sting.

Jellyfish parts

A jellyfish has a rounded body at the top, called a bell, with dangling tentacles underneath. Its mouth is in the middle, with armlike parts around it. Some jellies drift around, while others can swim along by squeezing their bell to squirt water out.

AWESOME!

The terrifying-looking lion's mane jellyfish is the biggest jelly in the oceans. Its bell grows to 6.5ft across, and its tentacles can be 200ft long!

Sailing ship jelly

The Portuguese man-of-war gets its name from a type of sailing ship. It has a gas-filled "sail" that floats on the ocean surface, stopping it from sinking. It isn't a true jellyfish, but it does have stinging tentacles for catching prey.

▲ Sometimes, man-of-war jellies drift together in the wind and get washed ashore.

Sea anemones

Sea anemones are related to jellyfish, but they stay stuck to rocks or coral. They reach out to grab food, such as small fish and sea worms. Like jellyfish, they have tentacles that can stick to and sting their prey.

▶ Sea anemones are named after the anemone, a flower found on land.

The Pacific Ocean

The Pacific is the biggest of all the world's oceans, covering a third of the globe. The word *pacific* means "peaceful"—but as well as calm waters, this ocean has plenty of storms.

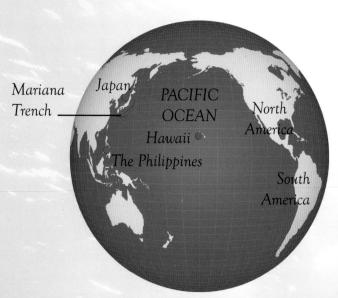

Mariana Trench ————

Japan

PACIFIC OCEAN

Hawaii

The Philippines

North America

South America

Floating feast

The Pacific contains a LOT of plankton —tiny plants and animals drifting in the water. Plant plankton float near the surface and use energy from sunlight to grow. Animal plankton often feed on plant plankton. Together, they provide food for larger sea creatures.

▲ The Pacific Ocean has many small islands and coral reefs, as well as vast areas of open water.

▼ Zooplankton is a mixture of very small animals and the early stages of larger ones.

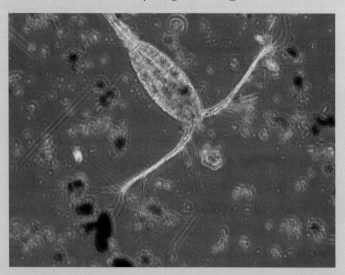

◀ A loggerhead turtle can travel at 15 miles per hour.

▶ Humboldt penguins breed on the coasts of Peru and Chile, in South America.

Currents of life

Currents are streams of fast-flowing water in the sea. Animals such as whales, saltwater crocodiles, and loggerhead turtles use the Pacific currents to swim long distances.

Cold current

As the Humboldt Current flows past South America, it sucks deep water up to the surface. This water is filled with chemicals from the seabed that provide food for plankton. Fish flock to feed on the plankton, followed by seals and seabirds.

Humpbacks of Hawaii

Huge humpback whales visit the cooler areas around the poles to feed on plankton, krill, and small fish. They then swim to the warm, tropical seas around Hawaii, Mexico, or the Philippines to mate.

AWESOME!

The Pacific Ocean contains the Mariana Trench, the deepest point in all the world's oceans. The bottom of the trench is almost seven miles deep!

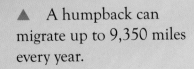

▲ A humpback can migrate up to 9,350 miles every year.

Along the coast

A coastline is a strip of land next to the sea. The world has more than 217,000 miles of coastline—that's almost as long as the distance to the Moon!

▼ A walrus rookery, where the adults raise and protect their offspring.

Coastal nurseries

For many animals, the seashore is a safe place to lay eggs. Turtles hide their eggs under the sand, while seabirds such as guillemots nest on cliffs, where it's hard for hunters to reach their eggs. Seals and walruses use the coast for their nurseries, known as rookeries, where the babies are safer from predators.

Dune dwellers

The wind blows sand into heaps, or sand dunes, which are often covered in tough seashore grasses. Animals such as lizards, snakes, and burrowing mice live among the dunes, feeding on insects or plants.

▲ Natterjack toads can lay their eggs in the warm, freshwater pools found on coastal sand dunes.

AWESOME!

While parents are fishing for food, fulmar chicks keep themselves safe by squirting predators with a jet of stinky, fishy vomit!

Seashore feeders

When the tide goes out, animals visit the seashore to feed on coastal sea creatures such as shellfish, sea worms, and crabs. Oystercatchers, for example, have specially adapted beaks for prying open shellfish or digging deep in the sand for worms.

▶ The tip of this oystercatcher's bill is pointed—perfect for picking up worms.

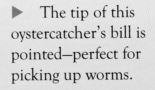

High and dry

At the coast, the sea moves up and down the beach twice a day, due to the tides. At high tide, the beach is covered in seawater. At low tide, it's left empty. So the animals that live here have to survive in two very different habitats.

▼ Mussels open their shells underwater to feed, but clamp them tightly shut to stay safe and damp at low tide.

▲ Mussels, starfish, crabs, and sea anemones are among the creatures found in tide pools.

Open and shut

Molluscs with shells are often found on beaches. Bivalves, such as oysters and mussels, clamp the two halves of their shells tightly together. Sea snails and limpets clamp the openings of their shells firmly onto a rock, and stay there until the water comes back.

Rock pools

On rocky beaches, seawater can get caught in cracks and hollows in the rocks as the tide goes out. This forms rock pools, or tide pools, where sea creatures can shelter at low tide.

AWESOME!

If you see a coil of sandy sediment on the surface of a beach, you've probably discovered a lugworm burrow. As the worm digs down, it passes sediment through its body and then ejects it to the surface. This is called a worm cast.

Under the beach

Even when the surface of a beach is dry, it's damp underneath. Seashore crabs and worms can hide under stones or in burrows in the sand. This helps them to escape predators and also stops them from drying out in the sun.

▼ Ghost crabs get their name from their ability to blend into the background and "disappear."

◀ Crab-eating macaques are found in Southeast Asia.

Mangrove forests

Mangrove trees grow on seashores in tropical regions, and they can survive being in salty water at high tide. Their roots stick up out of the sand or mud. The trees and their roots are home to lots of animals.

A place to hide

Mangrove roots stick out of the sand and act like a cage. Fish, shellfish, crabs, and turtles can hide there from hunters, such as sharks, while other sea creatures use the roots as a safe place to lay their eggs.

Swimming cats

In the massive Sundarbans mangrove forest, in India and Bangladesh, fishing cats swim after fish and crabs, and can even dive underwater to catch their meals.

◀ Not many cats like getting wet, but fishing cats are at home in the water.

▲ Male proboscis monkeys make a funny *kee-honk* sound through their long noses.

Mangrove monkeys

The crab-eating macaque feeds on fruit and crabs on beaches and mudflats. The funny-looking proboscis monkey swims around salty mangrove swamps in search of its favorite fruits.

Walking fish

Mudskippers feed on worms, insects, and shrimp that live in the mud around mangrove roots. To reach them, these strange fish can crawl out of the sea and hop along on the mud, using their front fins like a pair of legs.

▶ When out of water, mudskippers keep a frothy mixture of air and water in their gills so they can breathe.

The Atlantic Ocean

The Atlantic is the world's second largest ocean. An undersea mountain range, called the Mid-Atlantic Ridge, runs all the way down its middle.

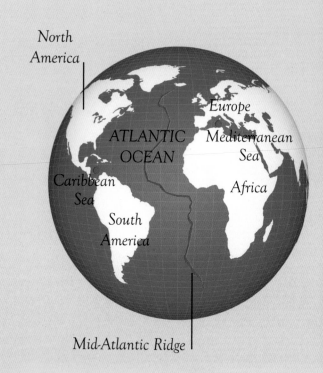

North America

ATLANTIC OCEAN

Europe

Mediterranean Sea

Caribbean Sea

Africa

South America

Mid-Atlantic Ridge

▶ The Atlantic Ocean includes many smaller seas and bays.

Dolphins on display

There are more than 30 species of dolphin. They often surf along the waves made by boats and ships, an activity called "bow riding." They can also leap right out of the sea, twisting, spinning, or flipping over in amazing acrobatic displays.

▶ Bottlenose dolphins can reach speeds of over 20 miles per hour.

◄ The Dumbo octopus floats just above the seabed to look out for prey.

Life on the ridge

Most of the Mid-Atlantic Ridge lies far below the ocean surface, at a depth of about 10,000ft. Dumbo octopuses have been found there. They're named after their fins, which look like the ears of a cartoon elephant.

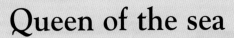

Queen of the sea

The Atlantic Ocean includes the warm, tropical Caribbean Sea. Here, there are lots of islands surrounded by shallow waters and coral reefs. Many beautiful seashells are found here, such as that of the queen conch, a very large sea snail.

► The queen conch's white and pink shell can grow to 12 inches long. People in the Caribbean often eat the giant snail inside.

95

The open ocean

The wide, deep part of the ocean lies far away from land.
It is also known as the "pelagic zone." There is plenty of
space here, so it's a good home for large, fast creatures
as well as much smaller animals.

Pelagic birds

Sooty terns and albatrosses can
spend years out at sea, landing
on the surface to catch fish.
Macaroni penguins spend most
of the year in the open sea,
feeding on fish and krill, only
coming ashore to breed.

▶ Macaroni penguins sometimes
swim more than 6,500 miles
in search of food.

▼ Sardines swimming
in the bright, sunlit zone.

Up and down

Scientists divide the open ocean into
layers, or zones, from top to bottom.

The sunlit zone
(0–650ft deep)

Sunlight shines into the water here,
so that plant plankton and seaweed
can grow as food for ocean animals.
The water contains lots of oxygen
for the animals to breathe.

The twilight zone (650–3,250ft deep)

There is very little light here, and the water is colder, so there are fewer animals.

 A sperm whale can hold its breath for more than an hour and dive down to over 3,250ft.

Midnight zone (Below 3,250ft deep)

Deep down in the open ocean it is completely dark. The creatures that live here often have bodies that they can "light up" naturally.

▼ Lanternfish are named after the bright spots of light on their body.

AWESOME!

There are very few large hunters on the deep-sea floor. This bluntnose six-gill shark is one of them. It scavenges for leftovers on the seabed by day, and creeps up to feed on living prey at night.

Ocean hunters

In the open ocean, it can be very hard to hide. There are predators everywhere, attacking from all directions.

Feeding on fish

The main food on the open ocean menu is fish. Shoals of sardines, capelin, anchovies, and other small fish are devoured by bigger fish, sharks, penguins, squid, whales, and dolphins.

▼ These lemon sharks have pale skin, which hides them against the sandy seabed as they hunt.

▼ The blue-spotted stingray has bright patterns on its skin to warn predators to stay away. It has two venomous spines in its tail.

Hunting with venom

Venomous animals inject killer chemicals into their prey, using fangs, spines, or tentacles. Jellyfish use stinging tentacles to hunt. This means they can catch other animals even though they are neither strong nor fast.

▲ A whale shark filters about 1,600 gallons of water every hour, taking small shrimp and plankton from the water.

Filter feeders

Some larger sea creatures move slowly, and have to catch fish a different way. Whale sharks suck in vast amounts of seawater, along with the plankton and fish it contains. Their huge mouth lets the water flow back out again, but keeps the food trapped inside.

On the move

In the open ocean, many sea creatures have to move fast to get away from danger, or to catch prey. Others must swim long distances to feed or breed.

Some animals have adapted to move easily through water. Creatures such as dolphins have a long, pointed shape that helps water to flow past them. Their power comes from flexing their strong, muscular tail.

▲ These sea lions are using their flippers to change direction quickly.

Flippers

The wings, fins, or legs of some animals have adapted to become flat, paddle-shaped limbs that are perfect for swimming. Flippers are also very useful for steering.

▼ The blue marlin is one of the fastest fish in the sea, traveling almost 65 miles per hour.

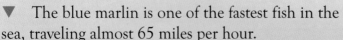

Unusual movers

Octopuses and squid have a siphon, which is a funnel sticking out of their bodies. They can fill themselves up with water, then squirt it out of the siphon. This pushes them forward.

To escape danger, flying fish paddle incredibly fast with their tails to launch themselves out of the sea. Then they angle their winglike fins so that they can glide like a bird.

AWESOME!

Huge sharks, whales, and rays launch themselves out of the water, then fall back down with a huge splash. This is known as breaching.

The Indian Ocean

The third largest ocean in the world is the Indian Ocean. It lies between Africa and Asia, and surrounds most of India. It is mainly a warm, tropical ocean with lots of coral reefs.

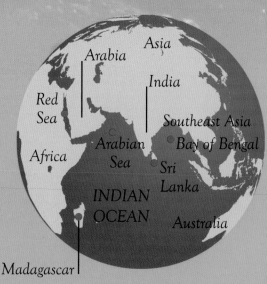

Warm waters

Warmer, tropical seas hold less oxygen gas. This means that the Indian Ocean cannot support as much plankton, krill, and fish as other oceans. However, many sea mammals and reptiles prefer the warm water, so there is plenty of life here.

▲ The Indian Ocean has many islands, including Madagascar and Sri Lanka.

◄ The lionfish is a venomous species found in warm, tropical waters.

▲ This clever mimic octopus, found in the Indian Ocean, can copy the appearance of other sea animals, often to avoid being eaten.

Shallow reefs

Many types of coral grow best in warm water, and the Indian Ocean has some incredible coral reefs. They grow near beaches and around islands. The ocean's reef creatures include the venomous lionfish, the well hidden spiny devilfish, and the cunning mimic octopus.

▼ The venomous spiny devilfish, or demon stinger, partially buries itself in the seabed during the day.

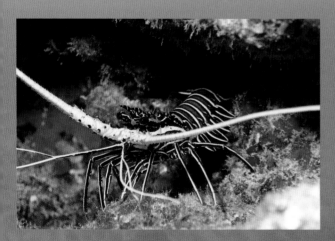

▲ Spiny lobsters inhabit tropical reefs all over the Indian and Pacific oceans.

Coral reefs

Reefs lie under the surface of the sea, making an area of shallow water. Reefs can be made of rock, sand, or coral, which is a kind of seashell made by tiny sea creatures called coral polyps. Coral reefs grow slowly, but can cover huge areas over time.

How coral grows

The polyps in a colony are linked together by tiny tubes, so that they can share food. Each polyp builds a hard shell around its base. As new polyps are born, they grow on top of the old ones. This is how the hard coral grows bigger and bigger.

▲ A coral polyp opening up to feed.

◄ Many different species of coral polyp can be found on one coral reef.

Coral reef dwellers

Coral reefs are full of life. The coral provides nooks and crannies where fish, shrimp, and molluscs can avoid enemies and lay their eggs. Reefs are also a place to eat. Seaweed grows on and around the coral, providing food for turtles, sea urchins, and crabs.

▲ Most octopuses are nocturnal, but the cyanea octopus comes out during the day.

AWESOME!

The Great Barrier Reef is a huge string of coral reefs and coral islands, about 1,500 miles long. It is the largest structure ever built by living things!

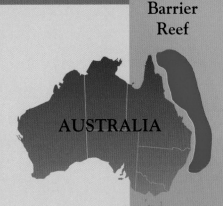

Great Barrier Reef

AUSTRALIA

By day and by night

Coral reefs form in shallow seas in warm places. During the day, the water is lit up by sunshine—and diurnal (daytime) animals are active. At night, these animals find places to hide or rest. Then the nocturnal reef-dwellers come out to feed.

▼ Hawksbill turtles are active during the day.

▲ This harlequin shrimp is a night feeder. Here, it flips a starfish over to feed on the soft tube feet and tissues underneath.

Living together

The different creatures on a coral reef live together in a way that helps them all survive. This is called an ecosystem. Other habitats, such as an icy sea or a mangrove forest, have their own ecosystems, too.

▼ The food web below is an example of a coral reef ecosystem. The arrows show the direction of the food energy as the animals eat other living things.

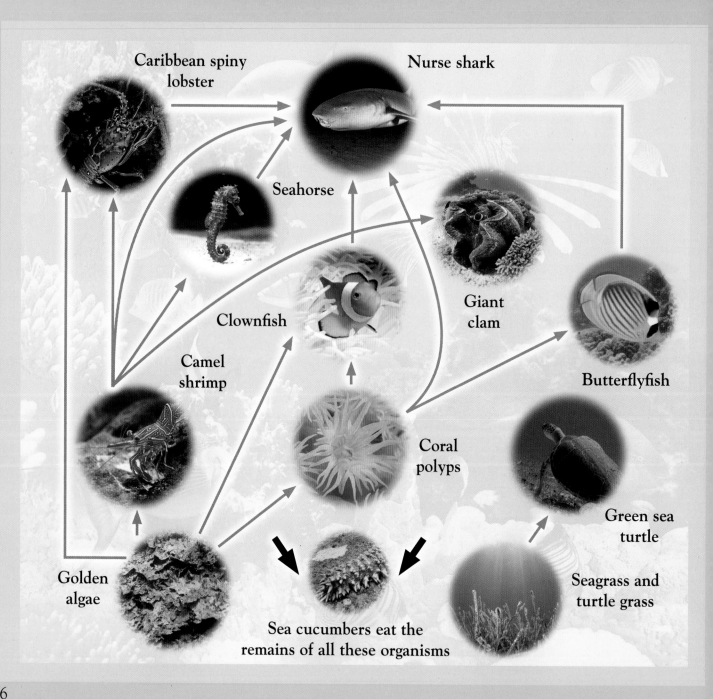

Caribbean spiny lobster

Nurse shark

Seahorse

Giant clam

Butterflyfish

Clownfish

Camel shrimp

Coral polyps

Green sea turtle

Golden algae

Seagrass and turtle grass

Sea cucumbers eat the remains of all these organisms

How does it work?

Because coral provides food and shelter, it attracts other creatures, such as small fish and shellfish. They attract hunting animals that want to feed on them, such as octopuses. Bigger hunters, such as sharks, then come to feed on them, too. The ecosystem ends up with a mixture of different creatures that rely on each other for food.

▲ A grouper lets a cleaner shrimp pick lice from its body and old food from between its teeth.

Helping each other

Two species sometimes live together to help look after each other. This is called symbiosis. For example, large fish called groupers visit areas where tiny cleaner shrimp live. The fish gets cleaned, while the shrimp gets a meal!

Scavengers

Who eats the animals at the top of the food web? When animals die, their bodies start to decay. Their remains get eaten by scavengers, animals such as crabs and sea cucumbers. In this way, the cycle goes around and around.

▼ A sea cucumber crawls across a reef, taking in bits of old coral so that it can extract tiny, living creatures from it as food.

The Arctic Ocean

The Arctic Ocean lies around the North Pole, the most northerly part of the Earth, and it's very cold. In winter, the ocean freezes. In summer, some parts of it melt.

Cold water life

The Arctic Ocean is icy cold, but it has a lot of plant plankton in it, especially in the summer. This provides food for other creatures. There are many fish, molluscs, dolphins, and whales. Humpback whales visit the ocean to feed.

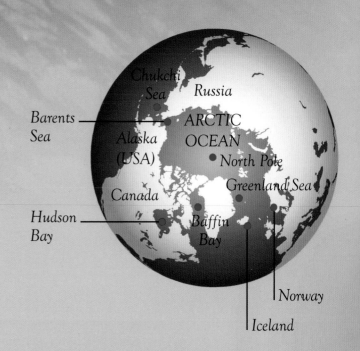

Chukchi Sea
Russia
Barents Sea
ARCTIC OCEAN
Alaska (USA)
North Pole
Canada
Greenland Sea
Hudson Bay
Baffin Bay
Norway
Iceland

▲ The Arctic Ocean is surrounded by Alaska, Canada, Iceland, Russia, and northern Norway.

◀ Beautiful, pale-skinned beluga whales live in the Arctic Ocean's coastal waters. They feed on fish and crustaceans.

▶ A hungry polar bear is looking for seals swimming below the ice.

Seal hunter

The plentiful supply of seals means a very large, fierce hunter can survive here, too—the polar bear. Ringed seals are the bears' favorite food. A polar bear will sit by a hole in the ice for hours, so that it can pounce on a seal when it pops up to breathe.

Land of seals and walruses

Walruses and seals are common in the Arctic. They dive into the water to hunt and rest on coastal rock or floating ice shelves.

▼ Walruses aren't very furry, but they have blubber (a thick, fatty layer) under their skin to keep them warm.

▲ Sunlight shines on the surface of the sea and passes into the water, to a depth of about 650ft.

Deeper down

Deep down in the oceans, below about 1,650ft, live some of the strangest, oddest-looking creatures of all. The water at these depths is extremely dark, and it is very cold.

Sinking snow

Plant plankton needs sunlight to grow. It cannot grow in the deep, dark sea. Deep ocean creatures use another type of food, called "marine snow," which sinks down from the waters above. It is made up of dead plants and animals, food leftovers, and animal poo.

▼ Japanese spider crabs can be almost ten feet wide and live at depths of up to 2,000ft.

Sea pigs

Sea pigs live on the deep, dark seabed. They are actually a type of sea cucumber, and are related to starfish. They feed by munching through the muddy ooze on the seabed. It is filled with bits of food from marine snow that has collected there.

▲ Sea pigs are not like real pigs. But you can see how they got their nickname!

Deep-sea scavengers

Hagfish feed on dead bodies. They release lots of slime to make themselves slippery, so predators can't grab them. They also use their slime to clog up the gills of hunting fish such as sharks.

Sea pens are plantlike animals that stand up from the muddy floor on deep ocean plains. They filter water to catch drifting bits of food.

The squid and the whale

The giant squid and the sperm whale can be found in the deep sea. This is especially amazing for the sperm whale, as it has to resurface to breathe air. It can hold its breath for 90 minutes to dive as deep as 9,850ft. It does this to hunt the giant squid.

▲ ▼ Giant squid can be up to 45ft long. They try to fight off sperm whales by tearing at them with their razor-edged suckers.

Shining lights

In the pitch-black ocean depths, the only sources of light are the living things themselves. Many deep-sea dwellers have lights on their bodies. Light made by living things is called bioluminescence.

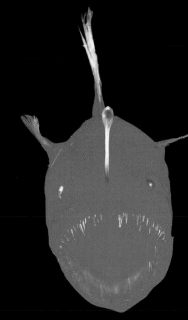

▲ A deep-sea anglerfish, on the prowl for prey in the dark.

► Copepods are tiny crustaceans, related to crabs and lobsters. Many deep-sea species are bioluminescent.

Lights as lures

The female anglerfish has a light on a stalk above its head, to attract other animals. When they come to take a closer look—SNAP!—the anglerfish gobbles them up.

I'm over here!

Bioluminescence helps some sea creatures to find each other in the darkness, so that they can mate and have babies. Some hatchetfish are thought to do this, as well as tiny, deep-sea crustaceans called copepods.

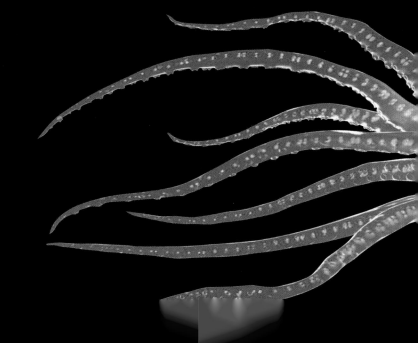

Most deep-sea bioluminescence is a blueish color. But the black dragonfish can make red light, which only it can see. It uses the light as a "secret torch" to light up prey, without the prey realizing!

▶ Many jellyfish, like this one, glow with a gentle, blueish light.

Flashing lights

Flashing lights—suddenly—can be a good way to scare a predator, giving smaller fish time to escape. One deep-sea squid uses the same method to confuse and stun its prey, to make it easier to catch.

▼ This pelagic octopus is one of the very few octopuses known to give off light.

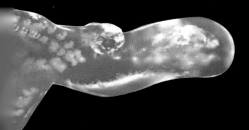

▲ The octopus glows from special suckers, arranged in rows

Glowing decoys

The vampire squid can squirt glowing, snotlike mucus from its arms. The predator chases this while the squid escapes. A similar decoy (a trick of distraction) is used by the bomber worm. It carries tiny, glowing "bombs" on its head. When attacked, it drops the bombs and swims away!

▷ Eelpout fish prey upon deep-sea copepods and crabs.

▲ Giant tube worms grow to more than 6.5ft long. Their bodies contain bacteria that feed on minerals in the water. They turn the minerals into food that the worm shares.

Vents and smokers

The inside of the Earth is made of hot, partly melted rock. In some parts of the seabed, water seeps into cracks and gets heated to boiling point, or even hotter. The hot water then bubbles back out through gaps in the seabed, known as hydrothermal vents.

Hydrothermal vents

Scientists first discovered the vents in 1977, in water 8,200ft deep, near the Galapagos Islands in the Pacific Ocean. They were amazed to see not only the hot-water jets, but also an amazing variety of living things around them that had never been seen before.

Black smokers

Some water coming from a vent contains dark-colored minerals, and looks like black smoke pouring into the sea. These vents are called black smokers. As the cloudy water comes out, bits of the minerals collect around the vents. They build up and up, forming tall chimneys.

▼ In this photo you can see giant tube worms and vent crabs on the far left.

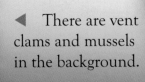

◄ There are vent clams and mussels in the background.

Eating minerals

Vent creatures do not depend on sunlight for their food. Minerals get dissolved into water as it heats up under the seabed. Bacteria around the vents then convert these minerals into food, which other vent animals can then feed on.

The Southern Ocean

Around the South Pole of the Earth, there is a large, freezing-cold continent called Antarctica. It is surrounded by the Southern Ocean. The waters here are icy cold, and often freeze over, but they are full of wildlife.

▲ The Southern Ocean lies around Antarctica and is surrounded by the three largest oceans.

Penguin colonies

Penguins are among the most common animals in Antarctica. The types found here include chinstrap, gentoo, King, and Adelie penguins. When they're not diving into the sea for food, they come ashore to mate, lay eggs, and care for their chicks.

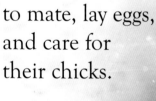

▶ A colony of chinstrap penguins can contain more than a million of them.

116

Crabeater seals are often found around sea ice, where they can easily go hunting for krill.

Even though penguin colonies are very crowded, penguins can find their mate and their chicks by their individual calls. The colonies are very noisy.

Get your fill of krill

The sea here is bursting with Antarctic krill. They feed on plant plankton, and on ice algae growing on the underside of sea ice. Lots of the animals that live here feed on the krill, such as crabeater seals, blue whales, and penguins.

Orcas prefer to eat seals, but will hunt penguins when there are fewer seals around.

Hungry hunters

Orcas, or killer whales, are common here. They grow up to 30ft long, have very sharp teeth, and hunt in groups. They can snatch penguins and seals from the water, or force them off the ice into the sea. Some orcas even surf up onto beaches to grab seals from dry land.

117

Oceans in danger

The oceans are big, yet delicate. Sea creatures need the right food and shelter, as well as water that's clean, not too hot, and not too cold. Sadly, humans have caused a lot of damage to the sea and its wildlife, and the oceans are also getting warmer.

▼ The scalloped hammerhead shark is endangered due to overfishing.

Overfishing

Our methods of catching fish and seafood are now so good that we are sometimes in danger of wiping out certain animals. Other creatures, such as dolphins and seabirds, also suffer by getting trapped in fishing nets.

▼ Oil floats on water, so when it leaks from ships it forms a "slick" on the surface. Marine animals can then get coated in it.

Pollution

Waste chemicals can flow into rivers and end up in the sea, making seawater dirty or venomous to sea creatures. Tankers sometimes leak oil into the sea, and the noises they make can confuse animals, such as dolphins, who use sounds to communicate and find their way.

◀ Global warming threatens to destroy the habitat of animals such as polar bears.

NOT SO AWESOME!

In the North Pacific Ocean, the swirling currents have collected millions of bits of plastic waste into a huge clump, known as the Great Pacific Garbage Patch. The plastic can make sea creatures ill if they accidentally swallow it.

Warmer waters

When certain waste gases are released into the atmosphere, they trap heat from the sun. This causes global temperatures to rise. As seas warm up, polar ice melts. This is bad news for sea creatures such as krill, polar bears, and penguins, as they need sea ice to hunt, feed, or breed on.

▼ Dolphins navigate and find food using "echolocation." They do this by making sounds and collecting the echoes as they bounce off objects.

What can we do?

People should never leave litter on beaches or drop it off boats. Many countries have now made it illegal to dump chemical waste into the sea, and are trying to encourage people to use less fuel and energy so that we can slow down the process of global warming. New laws help to prevent overfishing and protect endangered species.

A world of birds

Birds are amazing. There are more than 10,000 different species in the world—nearly twice as many as mammals (5,500 species). They dazzle us with their colors, songs, and flight. They also help to keep our world healthy.

Big or small?

The smallest bird, a bee hummingbird, weighs just 3oz—less than two paperclips—and would fit inside a matchbox. The biggest, an ostrich, is nearly 100,000 times heavier; at over 6.5ft tall it would probably have to bend down to get through your front door.

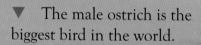

▼ The male ostrich is the biggest bird in the world.

AWESOME!

The Andean cock-of-the-rock is just one of the 1,820 species of bird in Colombia. That's more than any other country in the world and nearly four times as many as in the whole of Europe.

Everywhere

Birds live everywhere. You can find them in every habitat, from the top of the highest mountain to the middle of the driest desert. Emperor penguins are the only animals that can survive winter in Antarctica, the coldest place on Earth.

▲ During winter in Antarctica the temperature for emperor penguins can fall to –60°F.

Getting around

Flying allows birds to move around much more than most animals do. Many make long journeys, called migrations, covering thousands of miles every year.

▼ The Californian condor is one of the world's rarest birds; only 100 are left in the wild.

▲ A sooty shearwater may fly more than 37,000 miles every year around the world's oceans.

Birds under threat

People have caused at least 150 species of bird to disappear in the last 500 years. We have damaged the places where they live by cutting down forests, building cities, polluting seas, and introducing harmful animals into their habitats, such as rats. Today, around one in eight species of bird is in danger.

121

What makes a bird?

Birds are warm-blooded, just like mammals. But they can fly, lay eggs, sing, have beaks instead of teeth, and are covered in feathers instead of fur. While a few mammals can fly (bats) and even lay eggs (platypus and echidna), only birds have feathers.

Built for flight

Birds' bodies are specially adapted for flight. In place of front legs they have wings. Also, their skeleton is both very light and very strong. This helps them to stay airborne and to support the huge physical effort of flying.

▲ The feathers of this magnificent frigatebird weigh more than its skeleton.

▲ Nectar from a flower provides this brown-throated sunbird with lots of energy.

Energetic

Flying is hard work. Birds feed on foods such as seeds and insects that their bodies turn into energy very quickly. They also have a larger heart than mammals, to pump the blood more quickly around their bodies.

A lighter load

Birds' beaks are much lighter than teeth and jawbones. This helps when it comes to flying. A toucan's huge bill is one third of its length but just one twentieth of its weight. Inside is a honeycomb of air pockets.

▲ The huge beak of a toco toucan is much lighter than it looks.

▲ A goliath heron uses strong muscles to flap its big wings.

Muscle power

Birds have a much bigger breastbone, or sternum, than mammals. This bone supports the big pectoral muscles (the "breast" of a roast chicken) that power the wing beats. These muscles give them the strength they need for taking off.

AWESOME!

The ancestors of birds were dinosaurs called theropods, which lived on Earth over 65 million years ago. Birds' closest relatives today are crocodiles.

The wonders of wings

How birds fly depends upon the shape of their wings and how they use them. Some birds have short wings and flap very fast. Others have long narrow wings and prefer to glide. Many fly in special ways to help them find food or escape danger.

AWESOME!

An African vulture holds the world record for high-flying, at an incredible 37,000ft. That's 25 percent higher than Mount Everest!

Landing gear

Albatrosses have the longest wings of any bird. They glide low over the sea for hours without flapping. When they return to their nest, they lower their feet. This helps slow them down enough to land safely.

▼ A black-browed albatross lowers its feet as it comes in to land.

124

Built for speed

The peregrine falcon is the world's fastest bird. When chasing other birds it can fly at 155mph—as fast as a Formula One racing car. To reach top speed, it dives down and folds back its wings to make a streamlined shape.

▶ Pointed wings and a streamlined shape help the peregrine falcon to fly faster.

Flying on the spot

Hummingbirds can beat their wings at over 60 times per second, just like a buzzing bee. This high-speed flapping allows them to hover in midair. They can fly on the spot while sipping nectar from flowers with their long beak.

▼ This ruby-throated hummingbird stays perfectly still as it hovers.

▼ A mute swan flaps hard to take off.

In a flap

Big birds have to flap hard in order to get off the ground. A strong downbeat of their wings produces a force called thrust, which pushes them upward. Once they are airborne, they tuck their legs and feet back out of the way.

On land and water

Even though birds can fly, they still need to use their legs for getting around. Some hop, others walk, and a few are fast runners. Birds that swim, such as ducks and penguins, also use their feet to push them through the water.

▼ A greater roadrunner has strong legs for running fast.

Legging it

Birds that live mostly on the ground have strong legs. They often walk or run rather than fly. The fastest runner among flying birds is the greater roadrunner of North America. It can reach 25 miles per hour as it dashes after prey.

In deep

Wading birds, such as herons, have longer legs than other birds. This helps them go deep into water in search of food without getting their feathers wet. The longest legs of all, compared to body size, belong to birds called stilts.

▲ A black-winged stilt has the longest legs of any bird compared to its body.

AWESOME!

The African Jacana appears to walk on water. This water bird has extra long toes. They spread its weight and allow it to walk across floating water plants without sinking.

Paddle power

Many swimming birds have webbed feet. They use these as paddles to push them forward. Under the surface, some birds, such as penguins, also use their wings as flippers—just as though they were flying underwater.

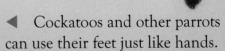

◄ Cockatoos and other parrots can use their feet just like hands.

Getting a grip

Parrots use their strong, gripping feet more like hands, clambering acrobatically among branches and often even dangling upside down. Their skillful toes can clutch food and lift it up to their bills.

Grounded

There are around 60 species of birds that can't fly at all. These birds are descended from flying ancestors, but they have lost the ability to fly as they no longer need it. Instead, they get around on foot or by swimming.

▲ The wings of a Galapagos flightless cormorant are too small for flying.

Bones and feathers

Flightless birds are built differently from birds that fly. They have smaller wings with smaller wing bones. They also have a smaller breastbone, and floppy flight feathers that are not stiff enough for proper flapping.

AWESOME!

The flightless cassowary is the second heaviest bird on Earth and weighs up to 130lbs—that's as heavy as a sheep.

Flightless island birds

Many flightless birds are found on islands. Wekas live only on islands off the coast of New Zealand. They are very inquisitive and eats all kinds of things, including lizards and the eggs of other birds.

▲ A New Zealand weka cannot fly.

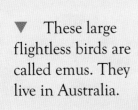

▼ These large flightless birds are called emus. They live in Australia.

Dead and gone

The dodo was a big flightless pigeon that lived on the Indian Ocean island of Mauritius. It had no predators until people arrived in 1598. By 1662 there were no dodos left. Today they exist only in artists' drawings and as a few old bones in museums.

▼ Dodos weighed up to 40lbs—as much as a collie dog.

Amazing feathers

Feathers give birds warmth, camouflage, display, and flight. They are made of a lightweight, flexible material called keratin, just like our fingernails. Tiny muscles allow the bird to adjust its feathers.

▲ The bristle feathers around the bill of this fiery-necked nightjar help it to catch insects.

Different jobs

Different feathers work in different ways. The large, stiff "flight feathers" on a bird's wings and tail help it to fly. Smaller body feathers keep it warm. Small "bristle" feathers around the bill of insect-eating birds help them detect their prey.

Warm and cozy

A bird's feathers keeps it very snug. Tiny fluffy feathers, called down, trap warm air against the skin, while larger ones form a weatherproof outer layer. Some birds line their nest with down feathers to keep their eggs and chicks warm.

▼ A female eider duck lines her nest with soft down feathers from her breast.

Feather care

Birds keep their feathers in tip-top condition by preening them with their bill or feet. They also take baths, by splashing in water or sitting in a rain shower. In dry places some birds shake dust through their feathers to dislodge dirt.

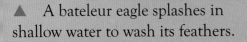

▲ A bateleur eagle splashes in shallow water to wash its feathers.

AWESOME!

The tundra swan has the most feathers recorded of any bird, at 25,216.

All change

Birds grow new feathers every year to replace their old worn ones. Some do it twice a year. This is called molting. Some birds, such as gulls and eagles, molt many times over several years before they acquire full adult plumage.

▶ A young herring gull (behind) is mostly brown; an adult is white and gray.

Showing off and hiding

As well as keeping a bird warm and helping it to fly, feathers also provide color. Bold colors can help a bird attract a mate or scare away enemies. More subtle colors provide camouflage, helping it blend into its background.

▼ A male peacock spreads his fan of feathers to impress females.

Look at me!

Some feathers are for display only. The fan of a male peacock, also called an Indian peafowl, consists of feathers that grow just above his tail, called tail coverts. When walking or flying he lowers them to make life easier.

▲ This greater potoo looks just like the dead branch on which it is perched.

Now you see me...

Some owls, nightjars, and other birds that feed by night have amazing camouflage. By day, their complicated markings perfectly match the background where they roost. This helps them to hide from enemies.

▶ The sparkling colors on this golden-tailed sapphire are an effect of the light.

Trick of the light

The sparkling blues and greens of many birds are made by the way light shines through their feathers. Other colors—such as black, brown, and chestnut—come from chemicals inside the feathers, called pigments.

▲ The male mandarin duck (on the right) is much more colorful than the female.

AWESOME!

The bright colors of some birds, such as this white-fronted bee-eater, may warn predators that they are not nice to eat.

Boy or girl?

Many male birds are brighter than females. This is especially true of ground-nesting birds, such as ducks, in which the dull feathers of females—which sit on the nest—makes them harder for predators to spot.

Grabbing a bite

Birds eat all kinds of food, from fruit and seeds to insects, fish, and even other birds. Each type of bird knows just how to find the food it needs.

◀ A red-billed oxpecker picks juicy ticks from the skin of a buffalo.

A helping hand

Some birds get help from other animals to find a meal. Cattle egrets feed around the feet of large animals, snapping up insects disturbed by their hooves. Oxpeckers go a step further: they feed on animals' backs, picking out ticks and other parasites from the hairy hide.

▲ A cattle egret searches for insects around an elephant's feet.

▼ A black heron creates its own shade for fishing in.

Fishing with umbrellas

The black heron has a special trick for catching fish. It stands in the shallows and stretches out its wings in an umbrella shape. When fish swim into the inviting shade, the heron snaps them up.

134

Waste disposal

Birds such as kites and vultures are scavengers. This means they feed on dead things or abandoned food. "Yuck!" you might think. But scavengers do an important job. By cleaning up garbage they help keep the environment clean.

▲ This whistling kite in Australia has found a juicy dead fish.

Bug snatchers

Many birds feed on insects. Bee-eaters catch stinging insects, such as bees and wasps. Woodpeckers chisel grubs out of dead wood. Flycatchers snap up mosquitoes, moths, and other winged bugs.

▼ A cicada makes a crunchy meal for this rufous-tailed jacamar.

AWESOME!

Jays are the memory champions of the bird world. During fall, one jay may bury 5,000 acorns as its food supply for winter. It remembers exactly where it hid them. Months later it digs them up again.

Beaks and bills

A bird's beak—also called a bill—is a special tool for feeding and finding food. Its shape tells you a lot about the bird's diet. Finches have a short, thick bill for crushing seeds, while eagles have a hooked bill for tearing meat.

▼ A kingfisher catching a fish.

Fish grabber

A kingfisher has a long, dagger-shaped beak. This helps it to plunge through the surface of the water and grab fish swimming underneath. It bashes the fish on a branch to stop it from wriggling, then swallows it in one gulp.

► Greater flamingos sieve plankton from a lake in Africa.

Upside down

Flamingoes feed on tiny water creatures called plankton. They use their beak like a sieve, swishing it back and forth and collecting the plankton inside. They always feed with their head underwater and upside down.

Cross-purposes

The crossbill gets its name because the two parts of its beak cross over at the tip. This makes a special tool for feeding on pinecones. The bird inserts its bill sideways between the scales of the cone and twists them open. Then it pops out the seed with its tongue.

▼ This crossbill is about to open up a pinecone.

AWESOME!

A puffin can carry more than 50 sand eels in its beak at once. Little spines in the roof of its mouth hold these tiny fish in place.

Big beak

The shoebill lives in African swamps. It uses its enormous shoe-shaped beak to scoop up prey from the water, including catfish, frogs, and even baby crocodiles. It then swallows its victim whole.

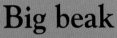

▶ A shoebill's huge beak has a sharp hook on the tip.

Working things out

Birds are very alert so it is hard to take them by surprise. They use excellent eyesight and hearing to find food, escape danger, and navigate safely in flight. Some also use other senses to tell them about the world around them.

Hawk eyes

Birds can see much better than we can. Their eyes are bigger than those of most mammals and five times more sensitive to light than ours. Birds of prey, such as hawks and eagles, use their strong eyesight to spot prey from far away while they are hunting.

▲ A sparrowhawk's powerful eyes can spot prey from a great distance.

Listen out

Unlike mammals, birds do not have ears on the outside. But owls do have especially good hearing to help them hunt at night. A barn owl can catch a mouse in the dark just by hearing a rustle in the grass.

Sniffing it out

Most birds do not have a very strong sense of smell. But for kiwis it is vital. These flightless birds are the only birds with nostrils on the tip of the bill. They poke around in leaf litter, using smell alone to find earthworms and other hidden food.

▲ A kiwi sniffs for worms at night.

Touchy-feely

Some wading birds have long beaks for poking deep into mud and soil. They can't see their food, but that doesn't matter. The sensitive tip of the beak can feel when it touches a wriggling worm.

▲ A painted stork feels for food beneath the mud.

AWESOME!

A hovering kestrel looks for trails of urine left by voles in the grass below. The urine shines with ultraviolet, a color that we humans can't see. It shows the kestrel just where its prey will pop up.

◀ A barn owl listens for rodents in the grass as it flies above.

Getting together

Spring sees birds singing, dancing, and displaying their feathers. Males do this to attract females so they can get together and breed. They are also announcing that they have found their own place—called a territory—so other males should keep away.

◄ A long-tailed widowbird performs its display flight.

Costume change

Some birds grow special feathers for display. Widowbirds live on African grasslands. The males usually look just like sparrows, but in spring they grow long black tail plumes and fly slowly around their territory.

▼ Male black grouse fighting.

AWESOME!

The male satin bowerbird of Australia builds a tall stick structure, called a bower, to attract females. He decorates it with bright blue objects, such as flowers, feathers, and even plastic litter.

Feathered theatrics

Some birds perform on a special stage. Male black grouse gather in a favorite woodland clearing where they strut, dance, and fight in front of the watching females. Each female chooses the male that impresses her the most.

◄ A pair of great crested grebes perform their weed dance.

It takes two

Some birds perform special dances. A pair of great crested grebes has a routine called the weed dance. They follow each other across the water, shake their feathered heads, and dangle gifts of waterweed.

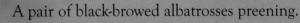

▼ A pair of black-browed albatrosses preening.

Staying together

Some birds go their separate ways after mating; the male, usually, leaving the female to do all the work of raising the young. Others, such as albatrosses, stick together for life. They strengthen their relationship with special rituals, such as using their big bills to preen each other tenderly.

Singing for success

About half of the world's bird species are singers. Males sing to attract females and to keep other males away. Songs vary from the simple two-note chime of a great tit to the complicated melodies of a blackbird.

A bokmakierie perches on top of a bush to broadcast its song far and wide.

Instead of singing, a great spotted woodpecker drums its beak on a branch.

Listen and decide

A female bird listens only to singing males of her own species. She works out from each one's song how healthy and strong he is. Then she chooses a male that she thinks will help her breed successfully.

Voiceless

Birds that can't sing may broadcast their message using a different kind of noise. A woodpecker finds a hollow branch and drums on it with his beak. The sound tells other woodpeckers that this territory is taken.

Song or call?

Songs are different from calls. A song is a performance given mostly during the breeding season. Not all species of bird can sing. A call is a shorter sound used for alarm or keeping in contact with other birds. All birds make calls.

AWESOME!

Some birds borrow songs and sounds from other birds. The marsh warbler, which lives in both Europe and Africa, imitates at least 212 different types of bird.

▼ A pair of bald eagles use high-pitched calls to communicate with each other.

143

Building a home

Birds build many kinds of nests. Some weave a complicated structure from sticks or grass. Others scrape a small pit in the ground or use a hole in a tree. The nest must provide a safe home until the eggs hatch and the chicks are ready to leave.

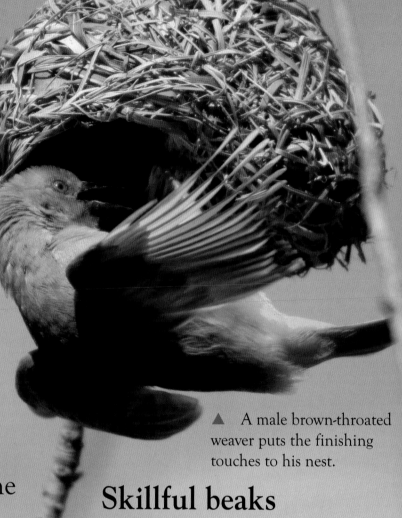

▲ A male brown-throated weaver puts the finishing touches to his nest.

Skillful beaks

Male weaver birds use their beaks to weave strands of grass into a perfect round compartment, with a neat entrance tunnel. They build several nests before the female chooses one that she likes.

Safe and solid

Some big birds, such as storks and eagles, build enormous nests that last for many years. They return each spring and add more sticks to make it stronger. Bald eagle nests may weigh more than one ton.

▼ In parts of Europe people provide special nesting platforms for white storks.

▲ A male Eurasian hoopoe brings food to the female in her nest hole.

The hole story

Holes make good nest sites for some birds. Those with strong bills, such as woodpeckers, dig out their own. Others may use an old hole made by another animal. Holes in trees, walls, and riverbanks all suit different birds. The Eurasian hoopoe uses a hole in a wall or tree.

Material needs

Gathering nest material is a full-time job at the start of the breeding season. The choice of material depends upon nest design. Some birds gather sticks, twigs, and grass. Others may use moss, feathers, and even spiders' webs.

▲ A male marsh harrier carries a stick to help build his nest.

AWESOME!

Sociable weavers in Africa's Kalahari Desert work together to build one huge nest. It measures up to 26ft across by 6.5ft high, and may house more than 300 birds in up to 100 individual compartments—just like an apartment for birds.

Eggs and chicks

Some birds lay just one egg. Others may lay 15 or more. Parent birds keep them warm until the chicks hatch, usually by sitting on them. This is called brooding. Birds that lay many eggs brood them for a shorter time.

▼ The eggs of a killdeer look just like the pebbles on which it nests.

Bare minimum

Many ground-nesting birds do not build a nest, but simply lay their eggs in a shallow pit. The eggs and chicks are camouflaged to look like the ground. This keeps them hidden from any passing predators when the parents are not around to protect them.

Breaking out

When a chick is ready to hatch, it chips its way out of the egg from the inside. The hatchlings of many birds are blind, naked, and helpless. The first thing they do is open their beaks and beg for food.

▶ Newly hatched garden warbler chicks beg for food from their parents.

146

Food supply

Parent birds work very hard to provide for their chicks. One pair of blue tits may gather 1,000 caterpillars a day while their chicks are in the nest.

AWESOME!

Ostriches lay the largest eggs. Each weighs 3lbs—more than 20 times the weight of a hen's egg. The shell is so thick that a grown-up can stand on one without breaking it.

▼ A female redstart feeds this baby cuckoo in place of its own babies.

Nest cheat

Some types of cuckoo lay their eggs in the nests of other birds. If the host birds don't spot the extra egg, they brood it along with their own. When the baby cuckoo hatches, it pushes the other eggs out. The hosts then rear this big, strange baby as their own.

Growing up

Some baby birds leave the nest almost as soon as they hatch. These eager youngsters can find their own food but still need their parents' protection. Once birds have learned to fly, they are ready to leave their parents behind and set off on their own.

Good to go

Ducklings leave the nest just one day after hatching. Birds that head out early like this are called "precocial." They are born with eyes open and fluffy feathers. Precocial chicks can get around and find their own food much sooner than the chicks of other birds.

▲ Baby mallards follow their mom soon after hatching.

▼ Great crested grebes ride on their parent's back.

Hitching a ride

Great crested grebes often give their young chicks a ride on their backs. The chicks are able to swim soon after hatching, but sticking close to their parents helps them stay safe. They also learn a lot from watching their parents.

Food parcel

Young birds do not know how to find food straight away. Penguins catch fish in the sea and feed it to their growing youngsters. After a few months, the chicks are strong enough to enter the sea and catch fish for themselves.

▶ A baby gentoo penguin takes food from its parents until it has learned to catch its own.

AWESOME!

A wandering albatross grows up more slowly than any other bird. It is not ready to breed until at least the age of 11.

▼ A group of baby ostriches is called a crèche.

Ostrich nursery

Several ostriches may get together to lay all their eggs in one big nest. Once the eggs hatch, the brood of up to 40 stripy chicks stick together in a group, called a crèche. One male ostrich looks after them all. The youngsters shelter beneath his wings from the sun and rain.

Living together

Many birds get together in large numbers. Some do this when they're breeding. Others do it when they're feeding, traveling, or gathering to sleep. A bird in a flock feels safe; it knows there are many more eyes to look out for danger.

Crammed in

Many seabirds form large groups, called colonies, to breed. Guillemot colonies are on steep sea cliffs. Each pair has just a tiny space in which to lay its egg and raise a chick.

▲ Guillemots pack close together on their cliff-top nesting colonies.

Safety in numbers

Snow geese gather in flocks of many thousands when they travel. They continually change position so that those at the center of the flock can rest while those toward the edge keep an eye out for danger.

▼ Snow geese travel in huge flocks when they migrate.

Sky patterns

European starlings gather in large flocks to roost (sleep). At dusk, before settling down, these flocks fly around the sky in tight, aerobatic formations. They look like swirling smoke.

▶ A flock of starlings swirls through the sky before settling down to roost.

▲ Red-and-green macaws gather to collect clay from a riverbank in the Amazon.

Extra minerals

Parrots in South American rainforests gather in flocks of several hundred to feed on the clay found in riverbanks. The clay contains important minerals that supplement their diet of fruit.

AWESOME!

The red-billed quelea is a small African finch that forms the largest flocks of any bird. Feeding flocks may contain more than three million birds.

Birds in forests

More different kinds of bird live in forests than anywhere else—around 7,000 in total, which is more than two thirds of all species on the planet. There are many different types of forest. Each has its own different birds.

Tropical plenty

Tropical rainforests are home to more birds than any other habitat. Rainfall and sunshine all year provide plenty of food. Most birds live high in the trees, and many have loud calls to help make themselves heard through the foliage. The biggest rainforest is the Amazon, in South America.

▲ The chestnut-eared aracari lives in South American rainforests.

◀ Capercaillies live in northern pine forests.

Winter survival

In far northern regions, such as Canada and Russia, the forests consist mostly of pine trees. Fewer birds live here than in tropical forests. In winter there is very little food and many birds leave. But a few find what they need. The capercaillie eats pine needles, so it can stay in the forest all winter.

▶ A tawny owl flies skillfully between trees to capture prey on the forest floor.

▼ A European robin perches on a garden rake.

Falling leaves

Deciduous woodlands consist of trees that shed their leaves in winter. In summer many birds breed here, but there are fewer in winter. Owls, such as the tawny owl, live among the branches and catch their prey down on the ground.

Forest substitute

Most of Britain's forests were chopped down a long time ago. But some forest birds have found a new home in gardens. The European robin once followed wild boars to catch any insects they disturbed when rooting in the forest floor. Today it often stays around gardeners for a similar reason.

Birds up mountains

Life in the mountains is tough for birds. It is hard to find food, and the weather can be very harsh, with strong winds and freezing temperatures, especially in winter. But some birds are specially adapted to thrive in these conditions.

▼ A bearded vulture circles, looking for bones.

▲ The Andean condor has the biggest wings of any bird in the world.

Soaring high

Big birds, such as vultures, use mountain breezes to gain height without flapping. The Andean condor soars above the Andes mountains in South America on its huge ten-foot wings. The bearded vulture of Africa and Asia, which is almost as big, smashes bones by dropping them onto the rocks, then swoops down to eat the marrow.

Creeping up cliffs

The wallcreeper lives in the high mountains of Europe and Asia. It is related to treecreepers, which live in woods. But instead of creeping up trees to find food, it creeps up rocks and cliffs, using its long, curved beak to probe into crevices for tiny insects.

▼ Wallcreepers find food on rocky mountainsides.

Mountain mists

When tropical forests grow on mountainsides, they are often smothered in cloud. This forms a habitat called cloudforest, where it is constantly damp and the trees are covered in moss. Some special birds live in cloudforest, including the resplendent quetzal, the national bird of Guatemela.

▶ The resplendent quetzal lives in cloud forests on volcanoes in Central America.

AWESOME!

The yellow-billed chough (pronounced "chuff") is a type of crow that lives high in the mountains of Europe and Asia. This bird has been seen living at a height of 26,500ft on Mount Everest—way higher than any human being can live.

Birds in grasslands

Grasslands are a habitat where grass grows naturally as far as you can see and there are very few trees. Big grasslands include the prairies of North America and the savannahs of East Africa. Grassland birds are adapted to living in the open.

◀ A skylark singing high above a meadow.

Singing high

Some grassland birds do their singing from the sky. With no trees to get in the way, they can broadcast their message over a large area. A skylark may fly up to 330ft in the air and sing nonstop for three minutes before it flies back down to the ground.

Blending in

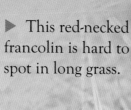

▶ This red-necked francolin is hard to spot in long grass.

Grassland birds feed mostly on the ground, which means they have to avoid hunters. Many have special camouflage feathers. Their colors and patterns look just like grass stalks.

Standing out

Great bustards are very big birds that live on grasslands in Asia and Europe. Their camouflage markings help them hide in the long grass. But in spring, males puff up their white under-feathers and strut around in a showy breeding display.

▲ A male great bustard puffs out its white under-feathers so females can see it from far away.

AWESOME!

The secretary bird stomps on snakes. It strides on its long legs through the African savannah, using specially tough feet to kill its prey.

Underground refuge

Grasslands don't have many trees or other safe places for nesting. Most birds build their nests on the ground or even under it. Burrowing owls in American grasslands nest in the unused burrows of animals such as armadillos.

▶ Two burrowing owls peek out from their hole.

Birds in deserts

Life in a desert is tough for any animal. It can be baking hot by day, with hardly any shade, and freezing cold by night. Even worse, water is often nowhere to be found. Not many birds live in deserts, but those that do have special ways to survive.

▼ Demoiselle cranes gather at an oasis in the Indian desert.

Desert journey

Demoiselle cranes migrate across Asia from northeast to southwest. Their long flight takes them over the deserts of northern India. When they get thirsty, they land at a waterhole. Many thousands gather to drink their fill before continuing their journey.

Budgies on the move

Budgerigars are tiny, seed-eating parrots that live in dry parts of Australia. They move from place to place. If rain falls in one area, large flocks quickly gather there and breed, getting all the food they need from the fresh new plant growth.

Sandgrouse are desert birds. Every evening they wade into a waterhole up to their belly, using special feathers to soak up the water. Then they fly back to the nest, where the chicks sip the water from their feathers.

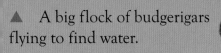

▲ A big flock of budgerigars flying to find water.

◄ Cactus wrens live on saguaro cacti.

Spiny protection

The cactus wren lives in the deserts of North America. It finds handy nest holes in the branches of the saguaro cactus. The cactus's sharp spines protect the nest from predators, such as snakes, which might want to eat the eggs.

Seabirds

▲ The southern giant petrel belongs to the "tubenose" group of seabirds.

Seas and oceans cover about three quarters of our planet. Lots of birds find a home out on the waves. Some live on coasts and islands, others far out at sea. Many breed in large gatherings, called colonies.

Less salt

Petrels belong to the "tubenose" family of seabirds. These birds spend most of their lives far out at sea. A special tube on top of their beak helps them to filter salt out of seawater. It means they can still drink fresh water out in the middle of the ocean.

Fresh to salty

Some birds spend part of their lives at sea and part inland. The red-throated diver nests on freshwater lakes but flies out every morning to fish in the sea. When breeding is over, it heads out to sea and stays there until spring.

▼ A red-throated diver catches fish in the sea.

Gannets are the high-dive champions of the bird world. They fold up their wings and plunge down into the sea like a missile to grab fish in their beak.

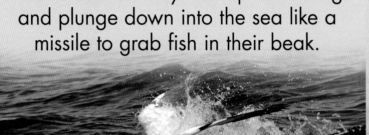

Fast flippers

Penguins live in the southern oceans. They are fantastic swimmers, using their wings as flippers to move fast through the water. Sometimes they leap right out of the waves for extra speed, just like dolphins do.

▼ Gentoo penguins are the fastest swimmers of all birds.

▼ Ruddy turnstones find food along the seashore.

Chasing the tide

Many species of shorebird travel up and down the world's coastlines, looking for food where the land meets the sea. They use their beaks to search for worms, shrimps, and other juicy tidbits under the sand and seaweed.

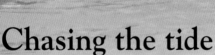

Water birds

Wetlands, such as rivers and marshes, are full of fish and other food for birds. They also offer safe nest sites, such as islands. Wetland birds have special adaptations, from webbed feet for swimming to sharp beaks for grabbing fish.

Fishing party

Many rivers in Africa shrink during the dry season, leaving fish trapped in small, shallow pools. Water birds, such as storks and pelicans, gather to scoop out the fish. These flocks are called fishing parties.

▲ A fishing party of marabou storks and white pelicans visit an African lake.

▼ A wading snowy egret shows its yellow feet.

Feet first

Herons and egrets have long legs to help them wade through water in search of food. The bright yellow feet of a snowy egret flash underwater and attract fish close enough to grab.

Ducking down

Many ducks live on lakes and ponds. Some dive down to feed at the bottom. Others tilt forward to lower only their front half. This is called dabbling. It helps them find food without going completely underwater.

▼ A pintail dabbling. It finds food just below the water surface.

AWESOME!

The dipper can walk underwater! It perches on rocks in streams, then hops down into the rushing current to search for food on the bottom.

▲ A bittern walking on a frozen lake.

Frozen out

Some birds, such as bitterns, live in reedbeds beside lakes and marshes. They usually stay hidden among the tall reeds. However, in winter, when the water freezes, they come out onto the ice to look for food.

Birds on islands

Islands offer birds safety from dangers on the mainland. Many are home to species found nowhere else. Some island birds are very rare; if their home is threatened, they have nowhere else to go.

▼ The knobbed hornbill is found only on certain islands in Indonesia.

Island variety

The 17,500 islands that make up Indonesia are home to 380 species of endemic bird. These are birds that are found nowhere else on Earth. Some amazing hornbills and birds of paradise live here.

AWESOME!

Imagine one big rock covered with 150,000 gannets! That's what happens on Scotland's Bass Rock every summer. With no land predators to worry about, this small volcanic island offers the seabirds a perfect nesting place.

Birds for mammals

The islands of New Zealand have never had any native land mammals. Birds have taken their place by adapting to living on the ground. Some, such as the takahe, have even lost the power of flight.

▲ The flightless takahe from New Zealand.

▲ The common cactus finch has a strong beak for poking into cacti.

Islands of science

In 1835, the famous scientist Charles Darwin visited the Galapagos Islands in the Pacific Ocean. He noticed how each island had a different kind of finch with a different-shaped beak. This helped inspire his theory of evolution, which explains how all living things have adapted to their environment.

Totally tropical

Todies are tiny, bright-colored birds found on the islands of the Caribbean. There are five different species. Each one lives on a different island and nowhere else. The Cuban tody, for instance, lives only on Cuba.

▶ The Cuban tody lives only on the Caribbean island of Cuba.

Birds in towns and cities

All over the world, towns and cities have replaced natural habitats where birds once lived. As a result, many birds have lost their homes, but others have found a way to survive in their new man-made environment.

Places for pigeons

The flocks of pigeons that you see in towns are called feral pigeons. They are descended from a wild bird called the rock dove, which lives on sea cliffs. Feral pigeons have adapted very well to city life. They find plenty of food among our leftovers and good places to nest under buildings.

▼ Feral pigeons at home in the city of Krakow, Poland.

▼ Cattle egrets gather on a garbage dump in search of food.

Down at the dump

Garbage dumps and landfill sites outside towns look very unsightly to us. But some birds find plenty of food there. Gulls that once lived only along the UK coast now also live inland because of the food they can find at dumps.

American goldfinches visit a garden bird feeder.

Garden benefits

Gardens can offer an important habitat for birds—especially gardens with lots of trees. Providing seed and other food in birdfeeders can help birds survive the winter in places where there is not enough wild food to go around.

AWESOME!

Imagine the world's fastest bird nesting on a skyscraper! The peregrine falcon has found a new home in the city on tall buildings, such as tower blocks and cathedrals.

Rooftop residences

Roofs make good nest sites for some birds. House martins nest under eaves, and chimneys provide a perfect platform for white storks. These birds fly off during the day to feed in fields, then return to their town nest in the evening.

▼ A white stork lands at its rooftop nest in Morocco.

Migration

Every fall many birds that nest in northern countries fly south to spend the winter somewhere warmer, where there is more food. These journeys are called migrations. Every spring they fly back north to breed.

On the wire

Swallows gather on overhead wires before leaving Europe on their fall migration to Africa. Before scientists knew the amazing truth about migration, people didn't understand where swallows went every winter. Some thought they hibernated at the bottom of ponds, like frogs.

▲ A flock of swallows gathers before migrating.

▶ Small birds like this sedge warbler put on lots of weight before migrating.

Fattening up

Migrating takes lots of energy. The sedge warbler weighs just 0.5oz. Every year it flies around 9,500 miles to and from its winter home in Africa. Just before each journey it eats as much as it can, almost doubling its body weight to 0.8oz. This extra fat provides the fuel its body needs for the long flight.

Summer all year

The Arctic tern migrates further than any other bird. It breeds in the Arctic and migrates to the Antarctic. This means it lives its whole life during summer time and sees more daylight than any other creature. In its 20-year lifetime it will fly about 1.5 million miles—the same as four return journeys to the Moon.

▲ The Arctic tern is a record-breaking long-distance migrant.

▲ A waxwing eating berries.

Follow the berries

Some birds only migrate if their food runs out. Waxwings from Scandinavia feed on berries in winter. If they finish their supply, they move on in search of more. Some cross the North Sea to arrive as winter visitors in the UK.

AWESOME!

A bar-tailed godwit once flew 6,800 miles nonstop from Alaska to New Zealand in just nine days. It probably flew very high, using strong winds for help.

Birds and people

Birds are very important to people for lots of reasons. They do important jobs for our environment, such as spreading seeds and catching insects. Watching and listening to birds also brings us lots of pleasure.

Caged colors

People have long kept birds in cages, to enjoy their bright colors or beautiful voices. Popular birds include different kinds of parrots and finches, such as budgerigars and canaries. In some parts of the world, though, birds have become very rare because too many are captured to keep as pets.

▲ The Gouldian finch, from Australia, is a popular cage bird but rare in the wild.

Watching birds

In the past people used to hunt wild birds. Today many people prefer watching them. Organizations such as the RSPB in the UK have nature reserves where you can see birds and other wildlife.

▶ People of all ages enjoy watching birds.

Pictures

People love pictures of birds. Some carry special meanings. For example, the bald eagle is the national bird of the USA, the robin has come to represent Christmas in the UK, and a white dove is a universal symbol of peace.

▲ The European robin is a symbol of Christmas in the UK.

▲ The red junglefowl is very rare in the wild.

Chicken ancestor

The red junglefowl of tropical Asia is the ancestor of the domestic chicken. Today there are more than 19 billion chickens in the world—that's about three per person— but the junglefowl is very rare in the wild.

AWESOME!

People used carrier pigeons to carry important messages between Britain and France during World Wars One and Two.

Birds in danger

More than 150 different bird species have become extinct over the last 500 years. That means they are gone forever. And today, one in eight of the world's bird species is under threat. Serious problems for birds include hunting, pollution, and cutting down forests.

Danger at sea

Seabirds are at great risk from all the garbage that people leave in the oceans. Fishing lines can entangle and drown them, litter can choke them, and oil spilled from oil tankers can clog up their feathers.

▲ A volunteer cleans oil off a guillemot.

▼ The Philippine eagle is one of the world's rarest birds.

Danger in the forests

People are chopping down forests to use the wood, or to clear space for towns and farms. The huge variety of birds that live in tropical rainforests are losing their habitat. Some, like the Philippine eagle, are in danger of extinction.

Danger from invaders

People have transported animals all around the world to places where they don't belong. These animals, such as cats, rats, and pigs, are known as invasive species. They can do a lot of harm to the native birds.

▶ Cats kill millions of birds in the UK every year.

▼ The ptarmigan needs cold snowy habitats, where its color helps it to blend in.

NOT SO AWESOME!

Moas were huge, flightless birds that could grow 10ft tall. People hunted them and cleared their habitat. By about 1400 AD moas were extinct.

Danger from climate

The Earth's climate is heating up. Scientists think that pollution from our cities, cars, and factories is causing global warming. Some birds that live in cold areas, such as the ptarmigan, are finding their habitat shrinking.

Protecting birds

Many people study birds and are working hard to protect them. They create reserves and improve the environment so birds can live safely. They also help the government pass laws that make it illegal to harm birds. You can help too.

▲ A skylark singing on farmland.

Farms for birds

Modern farming can cause problems for farmland birds, such as skylarks. They need wild grassland to find food or nest sites. Farmers are learning to reserve small strips of rough pasture for these birds.

Bringing birds back

By 1900 the red kite had become extinct everywhere in Britain except Wales. In 1989 scientists brought over red kites from Spain and Sweden. Now this big bird of prey is thriving—you can see it soaring all over the country.

▲ Red kites have been successfully reintroduced across England.

Finding out more

Scientists can attach a tiny, harmless ring to a bird's leg with details of where it was caught. This tells them where the bird travels. With this information, they can work to reduce the dangers that birds face on their journeys.

▶ The ring on this marsh warbler's leg may help scientists find out where it migrates.

AWESOME!

The crested ibis of East Asia was once the rarest bird in the world, but people worked hard to save it from extinction. Today there are more than 500 of these birds.

▼ The RSPB's Big Garden Birdwatch has shown that long-tailed tits are thriving in the UK.

Join in

On one weekend every January, people in the UK spend an hour recording their garden birds for the RSPB's Big Garden Birdwatch. The results tell us which garden bird species are doing well and which may need protection.

Glossary

Adapted Gradually developed to suit a particular purpose.

Algae Tiny, plant-like living things.

Amphibians Animals, such as frogs and toads, that have smooth, damp skin. Amphibians lay their eggs in the water.

Bacteria A type of very small, very simple living thing (made up of just one cell).

Bill Another name for an animal's beak, especially when it is long or flattened.

Bioluminescence Light naturally created and given off by some types of living things.

Birds Animals, such as toucans and macaws, that have wings, feathers, and beaks.

Breeding Having babies.

Burrow A hole, dug in the ground, where animals live or raise their young.

Caecilian An amphibian that looks more like a snake or earthworm. Caecilians live mainly hidden in the ground.

Camouflage Colors or patterns that help an animal to blend into its background.

Canopy A thick, green roof of treetops that stretches over the rainforest, beneath the emergent trees.

Captivity When animals are kept in wildlife parks or zoos – sometimes for their protection.

Cartilage A bendy, rubbery substance found in the skeleton of some animals.

Cicada A type of flying bug that makes a loud buzzing noise.

Cloudforest Type of misty forest that grows on mountainsides in tropical countries.

Colony Group of animals living together.

Conservation Protecting or looking after an animal, plant, or place for the future.

Coral A hard, shell-like substance made by coral polyps.

Coral polyps Tiny sea creatures, related to jellyfish, that live together in groups.

Coral reef A large coral structure built up by many generations of coral polyps.

Crèche Nursery group of baby animals, looked after by just a few adults.

Current A fast-flowing stream of water within an ocean, sea, river, or lake.

Decay To rot or break down.

Deciduous Describes trees that shed their leaves for winter.

Digest To take in food and break it down into useful substances for a living thing.

Display Special dance or show of feathers used in courtship.

Diurnal Active during the day.

Down Soft fluffy feathers close to the skin that help keep a bird warm.

Echidna Small, spiny, Australian mammal that lays eggs.

Echolocation How some animals use sound to find food or their way around. They send out sounds and detect the returning echoes.

Ecosystem A community of living things that interact with each other and their habitat.

Emergents A rainforest's tallest trees, which stick out above the canopy level.

Endangered In danger of dying out.

Endemic Native to one particular place and found nowhere else.

Equator The invisible "central line" that runs around the middle of the Earth.

Extinct A species of plant or animal that has died out forever.

Fangs Long, hollow teeth that snakes and some other animals use to inject poison into their prey.

Fish Animals, such as catfish and piranhas, that have fins and sleek, streamlined bodies. Many species of fish have scaly bodies.

Flightless Unable to fly.

Fresh water Water that is not in the seas and oceans – and is not salty – such as river water.

Gills Body parts used to take in oxygen from water, enabling the animal to breathe.

Gliding When an animal flies without flapping wings or other body parts.

Habitat The place where a species of animal or plant is found and is adapted to living in.

Hatchling Baby bird newly hatched from the egg.

Hemisphere One half of the Earth.

Hibernate How some animals rest through winter, when their body processes slow down to save energy.

Ice shelf A thick, permanent layer of ice attached to the land but floating on the sea.

Insects Animals, such as butterflies and ants, that have six legs and three parts to their bodies.

Invasive species Animal or plant brought by people to a place where it is not native and that often causes damage to native wildlife.

Keratin Hard substance found in animals that makes up horns, feathers, nails, and beaks.

Krill Very small, shrimp-like sea creatures that swim in huge shoals or swarms.

Mammals Animals, such as jaguars and orangutans, that have hair or fur covering their bodies. Mammals feed their young on milk produced by the mother.

Marine Describes things having to do with the seas and oceans.

Migrate To travel long distances, to find food or to mate and have babies.

Moulting When a bird's old feathers fall out and new ones grow in their place.

Mucus A slimy, snotty substance produced by many living things.

Mudflats Large, flat areas of seashore made up of mud or muddy sand.

Nectar A sugar-rich liquid made by plants and used as food by birds and insects.

Nerves Fibers in the body that sense things and carry signals around the body.

Nocturnal Active during the night.

Nomadic Always moving from place to place.

Nutritious Containing a lot of useful food.

Orchid A plant that grows in the rainforest and has beautiful flowers.

Organism Another name for a living thing.

Oxygen A gas that animals need to breathe, which is found in both air and water.

Pelagic zone The open part of the ocean, away from the coast.

Pigments Chemical substances that give color to an animal's skin.

Plankton Microscopic animals and plants that float in water.

Platypus Small, web-footed, Australian mammal that lays eggs.

Plumage All of the feathers on a bird.

Pollen A fine powder, made by plants, that helps to produce seeds and new plants.

Precocial Describes birds whose young leave the nest and feed themselves very early.

Predator Animal that catches other animals to eat them.

Preen How a bird cleans and rearranges its feathers, using its bill or feet.

Prehistoric From the time before humans began writing and recording things.

Prey An animal that is hunted and eaten by another animal.

Reef Any structure or object in the ocean, close to the sea surface.

Reptiles Animals, such as lizards and snakes, that have scaly skin. Reptiles lay eggs that have soft shells.

Roost Gathering of birds for sleep or rest.

Savannah Habitat with lots of grass in a tropical region such as East Africa.

Scales Small, overlapping flaps that grow from the skin of fish and some other animals.

Scandinavia Cold region of northern Europe that includes the countries Norway, Sweden, and Finland.

Scavenger Animal that feeds on leftovers and the remains of other animals' food.

School (or shoal) A large group of fish swimming together.

Sediment Material such as sand, mud, or slime that settles on seabeds and riverbeds.

Species Single, unique type of animal that does not breed with animals of other types.

Sternum Big bone in a bird's breast, to which its flight muscles are attached.

Streamlined Smooth and pointed in shape, for moving quickly through water or air.

Tail coverts Feathers (usually small) that cover the base of a bird's tail feathers, above and below.

Territory Particular area that a bird claims as its own, usually containing food or good breeding sites.

Theropod Member of a group of dinosaurs that walked on two legs and were the ancestors of birds.

Tick Tiny blood-sucking animal, related to spiders, that lives on the skin of large animals.

Tropical Describes things that are found in the hottest parts of the world, around the equator. The regions to the north and south of the equator are known as the tropics.

Ultraviolet A kind of light, found in sunlight, invisible to us but visible to most insects and birds.

Understorey The layer of rainforest plants and animals found beneath the canopy and above the forest floor.

Venom A poisonous substance that an animal injects into its enemies or prey.

Wading birds Birds with long legs, such as herons, that wade in shallow water to find food.

Warm-blooded Animals (mammals and birds) that generate their own body heat by burning energy instead of getting their heat from their surroundings.

Wildlife reserve An area that is kept safe and protected to give wildlife a place to live.

Zooplankton Tiny animal plankton.

Index

Picture Acknowledgments

Cover: All Shutterstock

Rainforests:
Insides: All Shutterstock, aside from the following images: p16 bottom left Mirko Raner/
Wikimedia Commons; p18 center right Stephen Dalton/Nature Picture Library; p23 center left
Lemurbaby/Flickr/Wikimedia Commons; p31 top right Rolf Nussbaumer/Nature Picture Library; p32
bottom left Dave Watts/Nature Picture Library; p35 bottom right Andy King/Wikimedia Commons;
p37 top right Pete Oxford/Nature Picture Library; p37 center right Bence Mate/Nature Picture Library;
p51 top right Nick Garbutt/Nature Picture Library; p51 bottom right Andrew Murray/Nature
Picture Library; p60 bottom right Roland Seitre/Nature Picture Library;
pp60–61 top center Doug Perrine/Nature Picture Library.

Seas and Oceans:
Insides: All Shutterstock, aside from the following images:
p65 center left Solvin Zankl/Nature Picture Library; p77 top right
Visuals Unlimited/Nature Picture Library; p80 top right Alexis Rosenfeld/
Science Photo Library; p95 top left David Shale/Nature Picture Library;
p97 bottom left Solvin Zankl/Nature Picture Library; p109 center left Doug Perrine/
Nature Picture Library; p111 center left British Antarctic Survey/Science
Photo Library; p112 top right David Shale/Nature Picture Library; p113 top left
Solvin Zankl/Nature Picture Library; p114 top Dr. Ken Macdonald/Science
Photo Library; pp114-115 bottom Dr. Ken Macdonald/Science Photo Library;
p115 right P. Rona/OAR/National Undersea Research Program/
NOAA/Science Photo Library.

Birds:
Photographs © Mike Unwin, as follows: p120, both; p121, center; p123, all; p124, both;
p125, center; p126, bottom; p130, top; p133, top left, top right, bottom; p135, top, bottom right;
p136, bottom; p139, center; p141, bottom; p144, both; p149, top right; p150, top; p152, top; p154, top;
p156, bottom; p43, center; p46, both; p47, center & bottom; p48, both; p167, top; p174, top; p175, top.
All other photographs © Shutterstock.